Recovering People

"It is rare to find a person who is both a skilled emergency physician and also a theologically trained ethicist. Here Quentin reflects on one of the most difficult challenges facing persons and communities in cities, that of addiction. But this is not dry ethics. It pulsates with the experiences of real people and with gospel hope and hospitality. His discerning, person-centered approach makes me hope that this is only the beginning of many books he will write on pressing ethical issues of our time."

—**Ross Hastings**, Sangwoo Youtong Chee Professor of Theology, Regent College

"In an age when Christianity is increasingly allied with cruelty to the marginalized, Genuis's brilliant, hopeful book shows the church how to be the good news of Jesus for addicted persons."

—**John Perry**, Senior Lecturer in Theological Ethics, University of St. Andrews, Scotland

"An insightful, warm-hearted, moving, but also appropriately demanding set of reflections on addiction—a comprehensive study of what addiction is, and what we can and should do about it. I warmly recommend this book, not least as a model of how to help people think in a distinctively Christian way about human personhood and its inevitable social and political entailments."

—**Iain Provan**, Emeritus Professor of Biblical Studies, Regent College

"If you find it difficult to locate trustworthy perspectives on addiction because it has become such an extensive, complex, devastating, and politicized phenomenon, *Recovering People* is a compass-like book that can help you get your bearings straight and chart a course in such tumultuous terrain. Not only is it written from the perspective of a medical professional who knows what he is writing about because he has the training and the experiences to speak from an informed perspective, everything shared in this book is framed theologically and composed with resonant levels of empathy and wisdom. In other words, I believe a lot of perspectives, and lives, can be changed by books like these."

—**Michael Morelli**, Associate Professor of Theology and Ethics, Northwest College and Seminary

"Addiction is one of the defining crises of our time. In *Recovering People*, Dr. Quentin Genuis calls the church to view those struggling with addiction not as problems to solve, but as neighbors to love. Writing with a rare blend of medical insight, theological depth, and lived compassion, Genuis urges us to bring Christ's healing presence to the wounded in our midst."

—**Kristin Collier**, MD, Director, Medical School Program on Health, Spirituality, and Religion, University of Michigan

"This is a beautiful and important book that grapples honestly with the strange and frightening problem of addiction. Genuis teaches us how to love our neighbor with addiction by teaching us to understand them. With tender and moving accounts of his patients' struggles with addiction, he exhorts the church to be the church, to be that 'immersive community' that embraces the prodigal, directs them to order themselves in Christ, and brings them 'purpose, new habits, and friendship.'"

—**Ewan Goligher**, MD, Assistant Professor, University of Toronto

"Quentin's words wrought in the crucible of experience are a tremendous gift to the church. In his personal model approach, he provides practical handholds for us to welcome, befriend, and love those in addiction. Quentin helps us transition from seeing people in our communities as problems to solve and instead he reminds us that our friends in addiction are peers created in the image and likeness of God."

—**Heath Meikle**, Urban Chaplain, Downtown Eastside, Vancouver

"Quentin Genuis's book *Recovering People* is the one book I would most want to put into the hands of Christians seeking to respond faithfully to addictions in their own lives and the lives of those they love. Genuis admirably combines careful scholarship on addiction with a physician's wisdom and bedside manner. This is a book full of empathy, insight, and hope."

—**Kent Dunnington**, Professor of Philosophy, Biola University

Recovering People
Addiction, Personhood, and the Life of the Church

Quentin Genuis

CASCADE *Books* • Eugene, Oregon

RECOVERING PEOPLE
Addiction, Personhood, and the Life of the Church

Copyright © 2025 Quentin Genuis. All rights reserved. Except for brief quotations in critical publications or reviews, no part of this book may be reproduced in any manner without prior written permission from the publisher. Write: Permissions, Wipf and Stock Publishers, 199 W. 8th Ave., Suite 3, Eugene, OR 97401.

Cascade Books
An Imprint of Wipf and Stock Publishers
199 W. 8th Ave., Suite 3
Eugene, OR 97401

www.wipfandstock.com

PAPERBACK ISBN: 979-8-3852-3123-2
HARDCOVER ISBN: 979-8-3852-3124-9
EBOOK ISBN: 979-8-3852-3125-6

Cataloguing-in-Publication data:

Names: Genuis, Quentin, author.
Title: Recovering people : addiction, personhood, and the life of the church / by Quentin Genuis.
Description: Eugene, OR : Cascade Books, 2025 | Includes bibliographical references and index.
Identifiers: ISBN 979-8-3852-3123-2 (paperback) | ISBN 979-8-3852-3124-9 (hardcover) | ISBN 979-8-3852-3125-6 (ebook)
Subjects: LCSH: Church work with recovering addicts. | Recovery movement—Religious aspects—Christianity. | Substance abuse—Religious aspects—Christianity.
Classification: BV4460.5 .G46 2025 (paperback) | BV4460.5 (ebook)

VERSION NUMBER 12/01/25

Scripture quotations are from New Revised Standard Version Bible: Anglicized Edition, copyright © 1989, 1995 National Council of the Churches of Christ in the United States of America. Used by permission. All rights reserved worldwide.

This book is dedicated to my patients and friends who suffer from addiction. The most important test of its value lies in whether or not it speaks about you in a way that is true, good, and beautiful. I ask your forgiveness for anywhere it does not.

This book is also dedicated to Grandma Potter, "GG," whose journey of freedom from addiction has given rise to the best things in my life. As she would say: "Hallelujah!"

All the stories in this work are true. I have changed names, along with some details, for the sake of clarity and for the confidentiality of my patients. Although this was a right decision, I feel grief at having done so. Their real names matter. The conversations and references to documentation come from my memory and so, of course, are not verbatim. Despite this, and even though I find it hard to believe sometimes, these tragic and bizarre and shockingly beautiful things happened. They are true.

A portion of the proceeds from the sale of this book will be donated to Jacob's Well, a "living room space" producing friendship and belonging in the heart of Vancouver's Downtown Eastside.

Contents

Acknowledgments | ix

Introduction: The Horror and Holiness of St. Paul's | 1

Section 1: What Is Addiction?

1. Framing the Question | 11
2. The Choice Model | 18
3. The Disease Model | 28
4. A Personal Model: Addiction as (Dis)Ordering Principle | 41
5. A Personal Model: Incontinence | 50

Section 2: Addiction and the Bible

6. Is Addiction in the Bible? | 65
7. The Parable of the Father's Two Lost Sons | 70
8. The Gerasene Man | 77

Section 3: Addiction and the Life of the Church

9. Refuge | 85
10. Nature | 95

CONTENTS

11. Repentance | 100
12. Order | 106
13. Belonging | 114
14. Recovery | 122
15. Hope | 138

Bibliography | 145
Subject Index | 151

Acknowledgments

LESS THAN A YEAR ago, my wife Kalyn sat cross-legged on our kitchen island with a pen in her hand and a single sheet of blank paper in front of her. "Tell me what you want to say about addiction." She scribbled as I rambled. That piece of paper became this book. My first thanks, as always, are therefore due to Kalyn. Thanks, love, for being my primary and most patient conversation partner and my best example of hospitality, loyal friendship, wisdom, good humor, and perseverance. Thanks to Michael Chin, dearest sir, for your tireless help and your belief in this project, even when I did not know what it would be. I'm grateful to have been part of the Providence Health Care family while working on this book. I'm especially indebted to the leadership and vision of Francis Maza. I am hopeful that this book articulates some of the personal vision for patient care that we seek to put into practice at Providence. Thanks to my teammates at St. Paul's, for a thousand night-shift conversations and for your grace in the thousand times I have failed to live up to the vision suggested in this book. Thanks to Kent Dunnington, John Perry, and Cara and Thomas Bergen for lending your considerable expertise in the many areas where I struggled to understand key concepts. Thanks to my models of cheerful moral clarity: Elise, Margaret, and Nicole. Thanks to Jon Bryars for the title and many other pearls of wisdom. Thanks to my other conversation partners, and readers, notably including:

ACKNOWLEDGMENTS

Lisa, Jake, Sam, José, Nicole, Tyson, Shelley, Jared, Sarah, Ember, Andrew, Aaron, Capri, Dave, Joben, Randy, Lori, Kai, and Chris. Thanks especially to Anisha Oommen for your precise and thoughtful help with content and referencing. Thanks to Ross Hastings for your encouragement and advice. Thanks to the community of Regent College, especially the students who suffered through my medical ethics courses and wrestled through these ideas with me. Thanks to Heath, whose loyalty to his friends in the Downtown Eastside is a heavenly gift. Thanks to the whole team at Cascade. Thanks to my siblings and their spouses, for the ways that each of you contributed to this project through our conversations on the subject. Thanks to my mother, Shelagh, always my first and best reader. Thanks to my father, Stephen, for being my primary example of a physician who cares deeply for patients as persons. Thanks to Josie Rose, for everything, really. Thanks always to Lila Christine, Rowan Taylor Alyosha, Elias Carter, and Junia Karis: how I love you, without knowing how.

The triage nurse asked me to see him right away because security staff were concerned about his "bizarre behavior." He was scaring the other patients in the waiting room. The triage team was not sure what his primary concern was: he had said something about knee pain, but he seemed scattered to them. I went to review his chart. "Past medical history of amphetamine use disorder: currently in the preparation/action stages of change," said a recent addictions medicine consultation note. Translation: he was really trying to get off crystal meth. "Cide" is what people commonly call meth on Hastings Street these days. I am not certain of the origins of that slang. I am not sure anyone is. But it seems tragically fitting to me. "-Cide" is, of course, the Latin suffix to denote something that kills.

I went to see him in the waiting room. The other patients had indeed given him a wide buffer of space. He was sitting in a chair, doubled over at the waist. His head was between his knees. His shoulders were shaking, his body writhing. He would roll forward so that his head sagged almost to the floor. Then he would tip back, white-knuckled fingers gripping his lower legs, pulling his feet off the ground. Then, forward again, his cheap shelter sandals slapping the floor as they came down. He was mumbling repetitively to himself. He was dirty. His thinning hair was slick with strong-smelling sweat.

"He was despised and rejected by others; a man of suffering and acquainted with infirmity, and as one from whom others hide their faces. He was despised, and we held him of no account."[1]

I sat beside him, putting my hand on his back to let him know I was there. I leaned forward to speak. And then, by God's good grace, I happened to pause just long enough to listen to him. "Dear Jesus," he was saying, "I don't need meth."

"Dear Jesus, I don't need meth. I don't need meth I don't need meth. Dear, dear Jesus, I don't need meth."

His body shook with the effort of prayer.

I should have asked him if he would consider blessing a sinner like me.

---

1. Isa 53:3.

Introduction: **The Horror and Holiness of St. Paul's**

MY WIFE, KALYN, AND I moved to Vancouver about five years ago. I had been accepted into an Emergency Medicine Residency program that was based at St. Paul's Hospital in downtown Vancouver. We were planning to stay for the year and then move back to where we had come from. St. Paul's is a large academic and research hospital. It is well known for excellence in caring for patients who live in, what is commonly referred to as, Vancouver's Downtown Eastside. The Downtown Eastside is a beautiful and historical neighborhood and its inhabitants have long been contributors to the artistic and cultural environment of Vancouver. However, more recently, the Downtown Eastside has been wracked by a multitude of complicated, tragic issues that are similar to the challenges facing inner-city communities in cities like Portland, San Francisco, and Los Angeles. The City of Vancouver website notes: "the Downtown Eastside has struggled with many complex challenges including drug use, crime, homelessness, housing issues, unemployment, and loss of businesses."[1]

In the emergency department at St. Paul's, these issues present themselves in the form of persons. A daily lineup of young people slumped over in orange plastic chairs after fentanyl overdoses.

1. Vancouver, "Downtown Eastside."

INTRODUCTION: THE HORROR AND HOLINESS OF ST. PAUL'S

A patient brought in by police with methamphetamine-induced psychosis, screaming and spitting and threatening staff members. A suicide attempt in a despairing patient who sees the hole of his recent relapse as too deep to climb out of. Another leg infection, this one progressing toward sepsis, in a patient who has been sleeping on the sidewalk since being banned from the shelters. A new HIV diagnosis in a patient too paranoid from meth to accept antiretroviral medicines. A phone call to a mother to tell her that her twenty-four-year-old child is dead from a presumed overdose. "How could you let this happen?" she screams at me, before dropping the phone and dissolving into sobs.

As a Christian whose vocation led me to work in this space, I believed—and still believe, more certainly now than when I began—that each of these persons was created in the image of the divine for the purpose of friendship with God, other persons, and the natural world. The God who feeds the birds of the air and clothes the lilies in the field cares for them. As such, each of these persons ought to compel my respect and even my reverence. My medical training had taught me it was best to be professionally distant and dispassionate. My faith, deepened through the study of theology, insisted it was right to be grieved and morally outraged at the suffering I encountered at St. Paul's, because of the significance of each person.

Often, the most grievous thing of all was an overwhelming feeling of powerlessness: a sense of total inability, despite the best efforts of our medical team, to meaningfully help our patients. I felt this grief most acutely when caring for patients with severe addictions to drugs. Their suffering grieved and angered me. It turned me into someone who cries in my car on the way home from work, something I never would have imagined when I chose emergency medicine as a specialty because I wanted to be the guy who put in chest tubes. And yet my grief and anger were not the reasons that Kalyn and I chose to stay in Vancouver when my residency year finished. They were not the reasons that led me to apply for a job at St. Paul's. What compelled me were the moments that revealed the beauty, dignity, and significance of the persons who were suffering

INTRODUCTION: THE HORROR AND HOLINESS OF ST. PAUL'S

in these ways. I felt utterly seized by the challenge of developing the humility and patience necessary to recognize and lean into these critical opportunities to learn, love, and care.

One such moment took place in the treatment zone of the emergency department, an area designed for addressing minor ailments. It was late in my shift when the triage nurse called and said: "I am sending a guy back there who thinks he has some glass in his foot. He has a violence flag on his chart and was very aggressive and irritable at triage. It might be worth having security on standby when you go to see him."

The patient initially lived up to her description. He was indeed aggressive and irritable, to put it mildly. But I managed to talk him down a bit. "I'm just pissed off because I have a bunch of glass in my foot," he told me. Understandable. I convinced him to let me have a look. As I did, I asked him what had happened.

"Well," he started reluctantly, as if he had done something to be ashamed of, "I used to be homeless, you know. There were a few months where I slept on the street in the Downtown Eastside and I did not even have shoes. I just wandered around in wet socks for days, trying to get money so I could buy more down [fentanyl or similar opioids]. But things are better now: I've got a place, and I've been clean for two months. I just started a job. Some guy there gave me two pairs of shoes: boots for work and sneakers for home. Today I was walking home and I saw a homeless guy sitting on the curb. He was high on something, just sitting there in the rain. He had no shoes. And I thought to myself, 'how can I have two pairs of shoes when that man has none?' I gave him my work boots and tried to walk home to put on my other shoes. But I must have stepped on a bottle or something." And so he hobbled to St. Paul's with glass in his foot and swore at the triage nurse when he arrived.

I find it hard to expound upon this story, as if I have an outside perspective from which I can view it. I am too close to it, too formed by it, to do so. I reside within it as a founding story for my own vocation. I try to see it everywhere, in everyone. Its juxtapositions and tensions are reflected in each of our souls. If my vocation produced no other goods, it would be enough for me to say that I have the honor of being the person who bears witness to the truth that this event simply happened. I also have the responsibility to be faithful to what I have witnessed by seeking to recognize similar acts of sacrifice and generosity whenever they are displayed by the persons around me. Particularly when they are difficult to see.

In short, what inspired me to work at St. Paul's, what makes me grateful and excited to go to work every shift, is the patients, especially those from the Downtown Eastside. Especially those struggling against severe addiction. I am blessed and challenged by witnessing their perseverance, humility, tenacity, patience, and hope. I believe that we can, and must, see these things without glazing over the deep challenges of their lives. The darkness is so deep, the losses so great, the sad days so unbearably sad, because the persons involved matter so much. The juxtaposition of the horror and holiness of St. Paul's makes the beautiful things shine with a special incandescence.

More Questions Than Answers

Both my moral outrage and my desire to respect my patients have made me passionate about engaging with issues related to addiction. Addiction is a catastrophe of our time, with devastating consequences to individual persons, families, and communities. By every metric I am aware of, personal and community harms from addiction have continually worsened over the past thirty years. This is especially apparent when we consider addiction to drugs, such as fentanyl and other opioids. In my own region, the "Overdose Crisis" has been a declared public health emergency for almost a decade.[2] Despite hundreds of millions of dollars and thousands of people working on the problem, overdose deaths continue to rise. A recent study suggests that about a third of American adults know someone who has died of an overdose.[3] Worldwide, it is estimated that ten thousand people die per day

2. See British Columbia, "Escalating BC's Response to the Overdose Emergency."

3. See Kennedy-Hendricks et al., "Experience of Personal Loss Due to Drug Overdose."

as a result of substance use.⁴ Each of these deaths is the loss of an irreplaceable person, the fracturing of a network of relationships, and the grievous wounding of a family and community.

Addiction is, of course, not just a problem in Vancouver's Downtown Eastside or other areas where its tragic consequences are visible to anyone who drives down the street. Behavioral addictions, including those to gambling and pornography, are increasingly pervasive in our society. Studies estimate that a near-majority of men in the Western world regularly view pornography.⁵ Further, addiction to pornography is widespread, if frequently hidden, within our churches. The consequences to individuals and communities are often devastating.

Addiction is an issue we must speak about, both because we are grieved and angry about the suffering it causes and, more importantly, because the persons affected are so significant. Each of them was created for friendship with God and for rich relationships of mutual dependence with other human persons and with the natural world. Addiction threatens the health of each of these relationships.

It is, however, difficult to speak of addiction. First, because the stakes are so high. In my experience, most people who come to the conversation have deep personal investment. For example, the first time I spoke at an academic ethics conference about addiction, there was a lineup of people waiting to speak to me when I left the stage. I anticipated a series of conversations about how I interpreted Aristotle. The first individual, a distinguished physician colleague, led with: "My son is an alcoholic." The next person had a brother who had died of an overdose; the next had a history of severe gambling addiction. And so it went, down the line. While each person had genuine intellectual interest, their commitments came from their guts: their deepest sorrows, wounds, and fears. My arguments about Aristotelian categories tugged on a thread that connected to the things that mattered most to them.

---

4. Grisel, *Never Enough*, 3.

5. See Wilson, *Your Brain on Porn*; and Regnerus et al., "Documenting Pornography Use in America."

Simply put, conversations about addiction are bound to be personal and sensitive. Addiction is too common and too destructive for it to be otherwise. One potential response to such a sensitive dialogue is to avoid the conversation for fear of saying the wrong thing and grieving our conversation partners. Such a response is understandable and often well-motivated. But I believe that it is not the Christian response. Part of our responsibility to love and serve our vulnerable neighbors is to learn how to enter these sensitive conversations well. To avoid the issue is to abandon the people who need our attention the most. We should instead seek to develop the creativity and humility necessary to inspire trust in our conversation partners, to affirm their need to be understood, and to bring humanizing precision to a dialogue that so desperately needs it.

This suggests a second problem: speaking precisely about addiction is challenging because addiction has been notoriously difficult to define. What exactly are we talking about when we use the term "addiction"? Most of us would instinctively recognize it in intense cases involving opioids, amphetamines, or alcohol. I suspect most of us would also agree that some behavioral patterns, including those related to gambling or pornography, can rightly be described as addictions. But we also hear frequently about addictions to social media and cell phones. We "binge-watch" our favorite television shows, and we speak casually about being addicted to work, potato chips, coffee, or running. Writers in the field of addiction research describe themselves or others as having addictions to classical music,[6] romance novels,[7] walks in the country, or love.[8] Are all of these really addictions? If not, where and how do we draw the line?

This leads to a third, related, challenge: Is addiction a distinct problem that affects only some, or is it a universal human condition that simply expresses itself in different forms in different persons? We often hear addiction described as a particular brain disease or

---

6. Maté, *In the Realm of Hungry Ghosts*, 104.
7. Lembke, *Dopamine Nation*, 14.
8. Schaler, *Addiction Is a Choice*, xiii.

disorder, especially in medical settings. On the other hand, many writers in the field of addictions research present it as a spectrum on which everyone falls. Christian thinkers have recently written books asserting that "everyone is addicted to something,"[9] and "we are all addicts in every sense of the word."[10] Who is right? Is addiction a particular disorder that only some people face, or a common experience we all share to some degree?

For Christians seeking to love and serve persons with addiction, there are also questions of how the Bible can inform and empower our approach. We do not find the term "addiction" in the Bible, nor do we encounter a single term or concept that has an obviously synonymous meaning. There are, however, notable passages in the Bible that describe experiences that seem to overlap significantly with those of addicted persons. Can you apply these texts to your own struggle with pornography or to your dear friend's feeling of despair after yet another relapse? Can we apply them in neighborhoods like the Downtown Eastside? If so, how?

Finally, the question of biblical interpretation should naturally flow into conversations regarding the life of the church and the role it might play in caring for persons with addiction. As we will see in the coming chapters, we often hear that addiction is essentially a medical problem and, therefore, solutions are to be found via biomedical research and medical therapeutics. One (unintended, I think) consequence of such a situation is that cultural and religious groups with potential to help often end up on the sidelines. Church communities do not want to set themselves up as an alternative to medical care for those with addictions. As a result, they often recede from the conversation, not from apathy or ill intent, but rather from lack of understanding of how to apply the life of the church to situations involving severe addiction. But is that a sufficient response from the community that hopes to be the hands and feet of Christ?

I think not, primarily because I believe the church is called to be a place of hospitality, friendship, and sanctification for

---

9. Zahl, *Low Anthropology*, 78.
10. May, *Addiction and Grace*, 4.

persons with addiction. Furthermore, both the overwhelming majority of personal accounts from persons with addiction, along with a growing body of research, suggest that certain kinds of human communities are necessary for healing addiction.[11] I believe that most Christians desire to contribute to the kind of social and religious spaces that produce grace-laden, mutual relationships capable of promoting healing for persons struggling with addiction. But how do we do so? Where do we start, if the problems of addiction are so overwhelming?

This book attempts to speak, from a Christian perspective, to our present addiction crisis, touching on each of the tensions and questions listed above. The first section addresses the foundational question: "What is addiction?" I will show how the most common contemporary answers, the choice and disease models of addiction, fail to say sufficiently precise and respectful things about human persons. It will then be possible to see, using the tools of philosophy and theology, how we might move toward a more nuanced and humanizing understanding of addiction. I will refer to this as the *personal model* of addiction. In the second section of the book, I will use two texts from the Gospels as examples of how we might bring our questions of addiction to biblical texts. In the book's final section, I will apply the insights of the earlier sections to the life of the church, landing on the ways that Christian communities can engage these challenging issues with grace and hope.

In other words, the three sections of this book present ways Christians might engage this urgent issue with our whole selves: minds, spirits, and bodies. The care of our minds, to seek a precise and respectful definition of addiction. The wrestling of our spirits, bringing questions of addiction into our reading of the Bible and our church conversations around freedom and hope. Finally, the labor of our hands, believing in the power of the Holy Spirit to transform our communities through our compassionate hospitality. As poet Christian Wiman has written: "Christ may be in us. But ours are the only hands he has."[12]

---

11. See, for example: Lookatch et al., "Effects of Social Support."
12. Wiman, *Zero at the Bone*, 41.

Section 1: **What Is Addiction?**

Today I stitched up someone's forehead. He told me that he had been minding his own business and someone had walked up and hit him with a pipe. I looked at his chart. It said something like: "Complicated post-traumatic stress disorder from early childhood trauma and severe polysubstance use disorder: opioids, amphetamines, benzodiazepines, nicotine, alcohol." No one had documented his tetanus status.

As I was stitching up his forehead, he looked at me and said: "St. Paul's is the only hospital I would ever come to." I asked him why.

"Not a lot of people care about east-siders like me," he responded. "But you people really seem to understand the people from the neighborhood."

He paused. I sutured and dabbed with gauze.

"In your own way," he went on, "you are like us." Then he chuckled and said he did not mean to be insulting. "No one wants to be from the Downtown Eastside."

I told him that I was honored, that he could not have blessed me more.

The longer I work at St. Paul's, the more it matters to me.

1. Framing the Question

I RECENTLY CARED FOR a young man named Jayden who presented to St. Paul's emergency department because he had an infection of the skin and soft tissue of his left leg. I had seen him a few times before, usually for fentanyl overdoses or infections contracted from intravenous drug use. Jayden is soft-spoken and witty. Sometimes I have overheard him giving health advice—well-intentioned, although admittedly of varying quality—to other patients. Once I heard him, again with the best of intentions, telling a patient with chronic leg wounds, "Just let your dog lick them and they won't get infected." Other times, I have heard him encouraging others to stay when they were thinking of leaving against medical advice and prior to completion of treatment.

On this particular visit, I asked him what had happened, and he told me the infection had been present for a few days. He said it started with either a spider bite or from missing a vein when he tried to inject "down" a few days prior. He had not injected much in his legs, but all the years of injecting in his arms had left the veins retracted and scarred. Hence, he was looking for new sites. I examined him and told him he would probably need several days of intravenous antibiotics. However, there were no signs of necrotizing infection or sepsis, so he could probably be discharged if he agreed to come back the next day for reassessment. Jayden said he would.

SECTION 1: WHAT IS ADDICTION?

Then I did something I try to do with every patient I encounter: ask an open-ended question to signal my care and willingness to help in any way I can, even with issues that were not initially mentioned. I sat down, to communicate that I was not in a rush, despite the back-up of patients in the waiting room. I put my hand on Jayden's knee, to communicate that I cared about him and wanted to do what I could to cross the distance suffering can create between persons. I said something like: "I am so glad I saw you today, Jayden. You are always welcome here. Is there any other way I can help you?"

He paused, then nervously asked if I could refer him to an addiction clinic. I told him that I would be happy to do so and asked him why. He explained that he had been injecting opioids for more than ten years. He had tried everything to stop, including medical therapies and extended stays in treatment centers. Nothing had worked. About a year prior, his mother had become very sick. His parents, who he had not had contact with for several years, found him somehow. In the weeks before his mother died, he stayed in their home and helped care for her. During that time, he stopped using drugs.

When his mother was "on her deathbed," she asked him to promise her that he would never use opioids again. He had promised. After she died, he stayed home, joined a recovery group, and worked on his relationship with his father. He had experienced more joy, purpose, and human connection in those months than he had previously thought possible. His words reminded me of a line from an addictions memoir I was reading at the time: "Being sober isn't just about not using. Being sober is about the joy a life of clarity... can bring. There is nothing greater than that."[1] For about ten months, Jayden had experienced hope and happiness.

Then he started using drugs again: "I just couldn't help it. I can't even remember why." He hid his opioid use from his father for a few weeks, but his infected leg and some missing electronics—stolen to pay for "some down"—had given him away. His father drove him to St. Paul's and told him, "When they discharge

1. N. Sheff, *Tweak*, 151.

1. FRAMING THE QUESTION

you, you need to find a new place to stay. You can't come home again." I sat quietly with Jayden after he finished his story. He shared feelings of shame, hopelessness, and entrapment. "I hate down," he said. "I *hate* it. I want to stop more than anything. But I can't stop. Why can't I stop?"

My faith tells me that Jayden matters deeply because God sees, knows, and loves him. He is a person for whom God became incarnate and so he ought to compel my respect and my reverence. Part of respecting Jayden means working to answer his question: "Why can't I stop?" In other words: "What is addiction?" Does Jayden have a chronic, relapsing, brain disease? Is it a trauma response? Is it a habit? Is his recurrent drug use simply a choice that reveals what really matters most to him, despite what he says? Does he have a genetic predetermination that renders him unable to resist the draw of opioids?

These questions are not merely philosophical. They have significant consequences for how I approach persons like Jayden: what interventions I offer and prioritize, where I send him for support and care, and how I engage with him in despairing moments. Moreover, our answers to these questions have profound implications for public health policy, medical treatment strategies, and indeed on the fundamental question of whether or not there is hope for persons like Jayden. Defining addiction is not merely academic musing: what we say about addiction has dramatic real-world consequences for vulnerable people in our communities.

When I started working at St. Paul's, I found it very difficult to integrate any existing model of addiction into my practice in a way that fit with my moral intuitions about persons like Jayden. Framing his addiction as a matter of simple choice seemed to cynically disbelieve his own account of his experience. Framing his addiction as a brain disease, a narrowly medical problem, seemed to miss the ways that the most important tools in recovery related to his story: his loyalty, particular relationships, and desire for a life of reconciliation and freedom. The event that prompted his longest period of abstinence from drugs was a promise that he made to his mom. Both "choice" and "disease" lenses on Jayden's story seemed to miss a piece of the explanatory puzzle. Both lenses seemed to look down on him, as either a depraved hedonist or a passive non-agent. I found I could not accept either.

The purpose of this first section is to therefore seek a more nuanced answer to Jayden's question: "Why can't I stop?" There are two dominant understandings of addiction that guide how people in our time think about this issue, the choice model and the disease model:

1. The choice model: emphasizes individual agency by claiming that addictive behavior is simply a matter of repeated voluntary choice. The choice model suggests persons continue in addictive behavior because they either value the behavior more than the risks or lack the resolve to stop.

2. The disease model: portrays addiction as a chronic, relapsing condition rooted in neurobiological changes that undermine free will. Behaviors that appear voluntary are actually driven by pathological processes, rendering the person *unable* to stop without targeted medical interventions.

We will critically evaluate these two models of addiction by asking two questions of each of them. First, does the model have precise explanatory and predictive power? Second, is the model adequately respectful of human persons? By exploring their strengths and limitations in meeting these criteria, we can better understand the challenges of addiction and the paths toward healing. This will allow us to articulate a more nuanced definition of addiction in subsequent chapters.

Explanatory and Predictive Power

Addiction, as demonstrated by Jayden's story, defies simple definition or easy understanding. Even those experiencing it often struggle to explain their own behavior. A robust explanatory model of addiction must navigate this complexity, providing clear and precise language to help individuals articulate their experience. It

1. FRAMING THE QUESTION

should also offer families and communities insight into aspects of addiction that seem bewildering or paradoxical.

For example, a robust model of addiction should be able to speak to the internal conflict that is a common feature of addiction. Persons with addiction frequently report competing desires: both a compulsive desire to engage in the addictive behavior and a sincere longing to stop. As Jayden said: "I want to stop more than anything. But I can't stop." The Diagnostic and Statistical Manual of Mental Disorders (DSM-V) recognizes this conflict as central to addiction, citing "a persistent desire to cut down . . . and multiple unsuccessful attempts to decrease or discontinue use" as a defining criterion. Philosopher Kent Dunnington has described this tension in the language of ambivalence. Using alcohol as an example, he outlines how people can see the thing they are addicted to as simultaneously good and bad: "good for drowning loneliness, good for summoning courage and so on; bad for spiritual well-being, bad for relationship to spouse and so on."[2] A nuanced explanatory model will account for this ambivalence by explaining the competing desires of the person. Doing so is critical because it can shed light on how caregivers can empower persons like Jayden to consistently act out of their deep desire for freedom from addiction.

A helpful explanatory model of addiction should also account for how addictions play out over time. A large body of research data suggests that many, perhaps most, people who meet the current criteria for addiction eventually recover.[3] Many of these persons do so without formal medical intervention. Furthermore, recovery often seems to involve the human will in a way that seems paradoxical. The individual's will seems, at times, to be powerless in the face of severe addiction. As Thomas De Quincey wrote about opioid addiction almost one hundred and fifty years ago: "The [person with addiction] loses none of his moral sensibilities or aspirations. He wishes and longs as earnestly as ever to realize what he believes possible . . . he would lay

---

2. Dunnington, *Addiction and Virtue*, 94–95.

3. See Heyman, "How Individuals Make Choices;" and Dunnington, *Addiction and Virtue*, 25.

down his life if he might but get up and walk; but he is powerless as an infant, and cannot even attempt to rise."[4] Yet Jayden's story reminds us that the individual's will can lend critical strength to those who seek recovery. His promise to his mother gave him the resolve to stop using drugs without any medical interventions. The human will seems to be both powerless and incredibly powerful in promoting recovery. A robust model of addiction should be able to make sense of this.

Respectful View of the Person

In addition to considering the precision of various explanatory models, we must also ask: "what do they say about the person?" To refer to someone as a person is deeply significant. When understood from a Christian theological perspective, the language of personhood orients us to the ways that we should love our neighbors both because of their differences from us and because of what we share in common with them.

To regard the other as a person is to see the truth that they are a being with potential for unique moral and rational agency. Every person bears the image of God, and every person does so uniquely through their own wondrous particularities of body, mind, and spirit. Bioethicist Gilbert Meilaender emphasizes how the language of personhood accounts for both our sameness and our individuality: "As human beings we share the characteristic human form and participate in its dignity, whatever our individual traits or capacities; as persons who always exist in relation to God, we are radically individual and equal."[5] To see the other as a person is to recognize how they are an irreplaceable self, created to actualize unique forms of friendship with God, other human persons, and the natural world.

To regard the other as a person is also to relationally affirm the deep things that we hold in common with them, regardless of

---

4. De Quincey, *Confessions of an English Opium-Eater*, 97.
5. Meilaender, *Neither Beast Nor God*, 102–3.

how different we may seem. Each person we encounter is a participant with us in a shared reality and a created human nature. Theologian Oliver O'Donovan points out: "The term 'person' too, must carry with it this implication of the old term 'neighbor,' that we find ourselves with somebody 'next to us,' like us, equal to us, acting upon us as we upon [them]."[6]

What does this have to do with evaluating explanatory models of addiction? It suggests that Christians should be critical of any model that fails to view those with addiction as whole persons: irreplaceable individuals who participate in shared humanness and have unique personal significance. A satisfactory model would account for our moral intuitions about persons like Jayden. There may be medical factors at play, but caring for him holistically requires engaging him as a person with a unique story—unique relationships, sorrows, gifts, and dreams.

Models in Tension

The next two chapters will examine the choice and disease models of addiction. The conversations around addiction in research, academic, medical, policy, and public settings endlessly revolve around which of these models is more precise and respectful of persons. These choice-vs.-disease model debates are becoming increasingly polarized, which is unfortunate because healthy conversation in this area is part of the task of loving our neighbors who have addictions. Oftentimes, the polarization results from the unexamined assumption that these are the only two options to explain addiction and from a resulting commitment to one of them without carefully thinking through all the implications of what it means. Other times, people pull from both of these mutually exclusive models to explain different features of addiction. Either way, the urgency of the situation demands a careful re-examination of both models in hopes of seeking a more nuanced model that can help us know how to more effectively listen to and care for persons like Jayden.

---

6. O'Donovan, "Again, Who Is a Person?," 367.

2. The Choice Model

What Is the Choice Model?

IN LATIN, THE VERB "addico" suggests being "given over," "assigned to," or "dedicated to" something or someone. Historically, this term had both positive and negative connotations.[1] The English term "addiction," derived from this Latin precursor, was probably first used in the sixteenth century and was initially a similarly "neutral" term: sometimes used negatively and other times positively. In Shakespeare's *Othello*, for example, Othello announces a party by encouraging "each man to what sport and revels his addiction leads him."[2]

In this original English use of the word, addiction meant a willful inclination or tendency toward a given behavior. Addiction was understood as a matter of choice and had little to do with compulsion. Sociologist Harry Levine explains how alcohol use, for example, was understood prior to the nineteenth century: "people drank and got drunk because they wanted to, and not because they 'had' to. In [this system of] thought, alcohol did not permanently disable the will . . . habitual drunkenness was not regarded as a disease."[3]

1. See Alexander and Schweighofer, "Defining 'Addiction.'"
2. Shakespeare, *Othello*, 2.2.
3. Levine, "Discovery of Addiction," 143.

2. THE CHOICE MODEL

Much has changed in the conversation since the nineteenth century. Common use of the term "addiction" has narrowed, taking on connotations of harm and more particular association with dependence on intoxicants. However present-day advocates for the choice model of addiction, although they might not use the term as broadly as Shakespeare did, want to continue to apply it in a similar way. For example, contemporary psychologist Jeffrey Schaler discusses addiction this way in his book *Addiction Is a Choice*: "A person starts, moderates, or abstains from drinking because that person wants to. People do the same thing with heroin, cocaine, and tobacco. Such choices reflect the person's values. The person, a moral agent, chooses to use drugs or refrains from using drugs because he or she finds meaning in doing so."[4] Oxford bioethicist Julian Savulescu, another defender of a choice model of addiction, claims: "addictive desires are just strong, regular, appetitive desires."[5]

In philosophical terms, the choice model of addiction is *voluntarist*: it suggests that addiction can be explained through consideration of the human will without inclusion of other potential causative factors. Accordingly, addiction is not even a particular phenomenon but simply is a label for willful behaviors that are repeatedly chosen by a person who has control of their actions. When these behaviors lead to risk or harm, the choice model suggests either the person's resolve is too weak to overcome their destructive will, or the person values the activity enough to accept the associated harm.

To return to Jayden's story, the choice model would suggest that, although he says the promise he made to his dying mother matters more to him than fentanyl does, his choice to use fentanyl reveals what really means more to him. Any claim that he "couldn't help it" is a misleading excuse. If we accept that his fentanyl addiction is bad for him, the implication of the choice model is either he is an incompetent agent—too weak to follow through on the

---

4. Schaler, *Addiction Is a Choice*, 20.

5. Foddy and Savulescu, "Liberal Account of Addiction," 15. Savulescu and Foddy call their model a "liberal model," but it is a kind of choice model.

promise he made to his mother—or an immoral actor—truly loving fentanyl more than his mother.

What's Wrong with the Choice Model?

In my view, the choice model of addiction is deeply flawed. It lacks explanatory power and is inadequately respectful of human persons. I suspect that almost anyone who has had a severe addiction, or loves someone who does, would not agree that ongoing addictive behaviors arise purely from willful choice. As Dunnington argues: "the choice model reduces addiction to mere weakness of will with respect to one substance or activity. In its more cynical mode, the choice model characterizes attributions of 'addiction' as a perverse psychological form of rationalization and excuse."[6] This simplistic approach does not accord to Dunnington's philosophical framework,[7] or to my experience. For example, I do not believe that Jayden's ascriptions of powerlessness, entrapment, and compulsion were mere excuses. It is more nuanced than that. Furthermore, the complexity of Jayden's situation is not exceptional. Most addiction is a result of multifactorial causality.

In my work as an emergency physician, I have cared for patients who were victims of human trafficking and developed addictions after they were forcibly injected opioids. I have read accounts of persons with sexual behavioral addictions who were first exposed to pornography when they were victims of sexual abuse. I once cared for a young patient who was first exposed to fentanyl at the age of twelve when her mother injected her as a "reward" for doing her chores. I recently cared for a young man who had no prior addictions but developed an "opioid use disorder" after he broke his leg and was prescribed sixty tablets of hydromorphone. He later overdosed and died in our ICU. In each of these cases, claiming the addiction can be explained adequately by considering *only* the will of the person involved is clearly missing several pieces of the

---

6. Dunnington, *Addiction and Virtue*, 35.
7. See Dunnington, *Addiction and Virtue*.

2. THE CHOICE MODEL

puzzle. In fact, evidence suggests that *most* people with opioid addictions in our time got their first opioids from a doctor for what was considered a genuine medical indication.[8] They did not begin using drugs simply because they wanted to. Their subsequent, often surprising and distressing, experiences of withdrawal and compulsion cannot be explained by appealing to pleasure-seeking or will alone.[9] The story is always much more complicated than any voluntarist account suggests. The development of addiction involves more than just the individual will.

Furthermore, from a Christian perspective, the choice model of addiction is not adequately respectful of human persons. It suggests that people have addictions because they are somehow weaker than others, or they are simply different morally speaking (this latter perspective sees the addiction as nothing more or less than a lifestyle choice). These accounts make assumptions that persons have addictions because they are weak-willed and that to speak of compulsion or entrapment is simply to make excuses. In its more cynical applications, the choice model can suggest that we have less responsibility to help those with addiction, since they are judged to be fully culpable for the harms associated with addiction. If duplicitous excuses are the only significant barriers between a person with addiction and recovery, then perhaps charitable efforts are best directed elsewhere. Having made their own beds, they can lie in them.

The problem with such arguments is not only that they miss a piece of the explanatory puzzle. They are profoundly and morally problematic. They place distance between myself and Jayden, suggesting that I should be looking down on him for relapsing rather than emphasizing how I should be looking across at him as a human neighbor and looking up at him when he shows remarkable loyalty and perseverance. They offend against the truth that my patients are neighbors from whom I can and should learn.

To share another example, I recently cared for a forty-year-old man with a severe alcohol addiction. He was far from home. He

---

8. See Lankenau et al., "Initiation into Prescription Opioid Misuse."
9. Foddy and Savulescu, "Liberal Account of Addiction," 3.

had come to Vancouver to seek recovery from addiction. Unfortunately, things had gotten worse in the years since he came here. He was beginning to despair, doubting that he could ever find a way to stop drinking. He had two names tattooed on his right arm: Evan and Christine. Christine stood out to me because it is my daughter's middle name. I asked him who Evan and Christine were. "My kids," he said, perking up a bit because every father loves being asked about his children. I asked him how old they were. "Six and eight," he said initially. Then, "No that isn't right." He paused, as if trying to remember something. "I guess they're eleven and thirteen now." He started to cry. Alcohol had stolen those years from him and from them. The choice model would say that he simply chose alcohol, that it *meant more* to him than those years with Evan and Christine. I cannot believe that. I should not presume that his love for his children is any less than mine.

To summarize, the choice model is conceptually simple. It suggests that addiction can be explained through consideration of a person's will alone. Therefore, other potential factors—adverse childhood experiences, genetic and medical factors, social and economic realities, political and cultural forces, or mental health—do not contribute. Psychiatrist Theodore Dalrymple summarizes this perspective: "When you consider what heroin addicts actually have to do to become heroin addicts it is clear that . . . they *want* to be heroin addicts."[10] It is unsurprising that those who work closely with people with addiction commonly reject this explanation and seek a more precise, compassionate, and personalizing model of care.

What Can We Learn from the Choice Model?

When I was studying for my master's degree, my supervisor frequently told me: "The role of a scholar is to help conversations go well." Being young and very early in my academic journey, I instinctively disagreed. "The role of a scholar is to win debates!" I

---

10. Dalrymple, "Stigma and Sympathy." Emphasis is Dalrymple's.

might have said. In the intervening years, however, I have learned that I must seek to enter conversations humbly and creatively, especially when those conversations are sensitive or polarized. A key tool for such a task, often disincentivized in the "us vs. them" social-media-mob debates of our time, is the ability to identify the good features of those arguments with which we strongly disagree. In other words, it strengthens our ability to know what is really wrong with an idea when we put our finger exactly on what might be right with it.

There are, of course, arguments that are entirely faulty and from which we can learn nothing. At some points in my life, driven by my moral indignation at some of its implications, I have been tempted to see the choice model of addiction in this way. But, despite its significant flaws, I believe there are three primary things that Christians can take from this model. First, we should have a high view of the agency of a person with addiction, particularly when we talk about healing and recovery. Second, we should consider the ways that addiction is a relatable phenomenon. And third, we should be willing to engage questions of meaning when we talk about addiction.

Agency

Given what I have said in the previous section, it might be all too simple to assume that "choice model people" are out-dated, cold-hearted moralizers who congratulate themselves after yelling "Get a job!" at the man sitting on the sidewalk asking for change. In my experience, this is not the case. Many proponents of the choice model care deeply about those with addiction and work hard to help them find healing and recovery. Most people who defend the choice model seek nuanced explanations and respectful language about persons with addiction. Why, then, are they attached to a model that is laden with problems?

In my experience, the answer has a lot to do with a desire to assert the *agency* of persons with addiction. To be a moral agent is to have the capacity to act with reference to the good, to be able to make decisions that promote what is healthy and right. Defenders of the choice model are concerned that the disease model of addiction suggests that persons with addiction have no agency. Savulescu, for example, asserts: "The Disease View makes a claim about what addicts can and cannot do. It claims that they cannot prefer to abstain."[11]

But we know, and choice-model advocates want us to remember, that persons like Jayden do choose to abstain at times. Moreover, in these choices, they demonstrate courage, love, perseverance, and patience. These are rich virtues and many of my patients display them in surprising, but nonetheless amazing ways. They enlarge my conception of the forms that virtue can take and convict me of my own need to grow. I would passionately resist any narrative of addiction that obscured my patients' beautiful human efforts and achievements by casting them simply as passive victims, non-agents. In this respect, I can relate to the passion of those who defend the choice model. Encouraging and believing in the agency of a person who feels trapped can be incredibly powerful. A richer understanding of addiction would avoid the problems of a simple choice model, but also affirm that persons with addiction remain agents. Their will alone may not be enough to produce healing. Nevertheless, the potential power of their agency is a good, God-given, necessary part of the process.

Relatability

Gabor Maté's *In the Realm of Hungry Ghosts* is one of the most popular books on addiction published in the past twenty years. Maté is a physician who worked in the Downtown Eastside of Vancouver. His book includes several detailed, often deeply tragic, accounts of opioid addiction and the harms that are caused by it. It also includes a chapter entitled "Takes One to Know One," wherein Maté describes himself as having an addiction to classical music that is comparable "along a continuum" with addiction to

---

11. Foddy and Savulescu, "Liberal Account of Addiction," 10.

2. THE CHOICE MODEL

heroin.[12] Maté asserts that, although there are differences between buying too many sonatas and injecting opioids, there are illuminating similarities. In both cases the individual experiences obsessive loss of free control, and both involve similar neurochemical pathways.[13]

Maté has been criticized for making this argument, and it is easy to understand why it could come across as insensitive. The dissimilarity of proportion in comparing "Beethoven-addiction" to heroin addiction cannot be overstated. There is something imprecise about suggesting a simple parallel between these behaviors. A richer model of addiction would be able to pinpoint exactly where this imprecision lies. A richer model would also be able to account for what is valuable about such comparisons: the assertion that addictive behaviors are relatable. Maté is attempting to explain how and why he can relate to his patients, especially those who seem very different from him. He knows how difficult it is to change his music-buying behavior. He tries to leverage this self-knowledge to produce empathy and respect for his heroin-addicted patients. Maté wants to say that his patients are *like him*. This instinct is admirable and critically important to understanding and caring for persons like Jayden.

Similarly, a charitable Christian reading of the choice model can affirm its emphasis on the commonalities that addicted persons share with all persons. Underneath our dissimilarities lie our relatable similarities: our frailty, our wounded nature, our need for mercy and grace. Especially when their actions seem difficult to understand, it is fruitful to lean into the many ways that we can relate to persons with addiction as a way of promoting mutual learning and mutual growth.

---

12. Maté, *In the Realm of Hungry Ghosts*, 104.
13. Maté, *In the Realm of Hungry Ghosts*, 109.

Meaning

I recently cared for a patient who, because of bizarre behavior and agitation, was brought to the emergency department by police officers. The patient had an addiction to methamphetamines. On the evening that I cared for him, he had used "-cide" and subsequently was seen wandering in traffic on a major city street. He assaulted an elderly woman sitting at a bus stop and then began banging his head against a concrete wall. Police officers were called and they found him to be "aggressive and disorganized." Recognizing that he may need medical care, they brought him to the emergency department. When I first assessed him, he was attempting to assault members of our staff team. He was shouting violent threats. One of the medical students, standing at the bedside, leaned toward the person next to him and said: "I can't imagine why anyone would ever do meth." The patient heard. He stopped shouting and flailing. He looked at the student and responded indignantly: "Yes you can! You can imagine it. I do it because it feels so, so good. You will never feel this good."

I keep mulling this encounter over in my mind. It reads like a scene out of Dostoevsky, Flannery O'Connor, or the book of Ezekiel. Truth comes to us from the source we would least expect it, orienting and convicting us. At the risk of over-interpreting, I believe that the patient, even in his altered state, was grieved by the implication that his behavior was incomprehensible. All our prior attempts to "verbally de-escalate" him had failed. What oriented him was the assertion, offensive to him, that his use of amphetamines was *meaning-less*. He challenged us to look closely at him, to see the goods he was seeking in amphetamines and not just the obvious harms.

To give the choice model of addiction the most charitable possible reading is to understand that it points us toward this same insight. It is conceptually simple and depersonalizing to say that people engage in addictive behaviors because they have a brain disease placing them outside the realm of rational or meaningful

2. THE CHOICE MODEL

decision-making. We should preserve the more complicated truth: addiction can be a way of seeking real human goods.

Looking at addiction through this lens helps us understand why addiction is so common in societies marked by individualism and the accordant loss of purpose and meaning.[14] From the memoir of a person with alcohol addiction:

> The search for a fix, for a ready solution to what ails, has become . . . an ingrained part of consumer culture . . . . In some ways alcoholism is the perfect [contemporary] expression of that particular brand of searching, an extreme expression of the way so many of us are taught to confront deep yearnings. Fill it up, fill it up, fill it up. Fill up the emptiness; fill up what feels like a pit of loneliness and terror and rage; please, just take it away, now.[15]

To put it simply: addictions *are* often ways of looking for the good things in life, including meaning. They are bad for persons because they ultimately fail to deliver the goods that they offer. For the Christian, this is a hopeful understanding. It suggests that, underneath the harms of addiction, persons are longing for the good things that can be found in friendship with God. For example, pornography harms you because, among other things, it fails to deliver the closeness and intimacy you were made for. But God wants to give you the good things you sought in pornography, and so much more. From another memoir: "Heroin offers safety . . . but it robs you of the possibilities that make holding onto life worthwhile in the first place."[16] But God wants to give you the good things you sought in heroin, and so much more. We will return to the beauty of this truth, but it will first be necessary to explore the neurochemical waters of the disease model of addiction.

---

14. See Alexander, *Globalization of Addiction*.
15. Knapp, *Drinking: A Love Story*, 60–61.
16. Marlowe, *How to Stop Time*, 297.

3. The Disease Model

What Is the Disease Model?

I RECENTLY TOOK MY daughter to a birthday party at a community center in Vancouver. I stood outside the gym and read the public noticeboard while the kids tried to push the bouncy castle over. Amid the advertisements for mindfulness consultations and kombucha-infusing classes was a notice sponsored by the Province of British Columbia. It read: "Addiction is a medical condition—not a choice. Stop the Stigma." The last three words were bolded. I went to the website suggested by the notice. The message was reiterated: "Addiction is a health condition—*it is the result of external factors, not personal choices.*"[1]

This notice succinctly captures the essence of the disease model of addiction, sometimes called the "biological," "brain," or "medical" model. The disease model is *determinist*, philosophically speaking. It occupies the opposite pole from the choice model in terms of explaining how the affected person's will relates to their behavior. The choice model suggests that the individual will is the only relevant causative factor in the development of addiction. The disease model asserts the opposite: that the will is not a perpetuating factor at all. This framework suggests that addictive behavior

---

1. Government of British Columbia, "Stop Overdose." Emphasis is theirs.

3. THE DISEASE MODEL

arises from a physical disease state that is not significantly different from conditions like diabetes or coronary artery disease.

As evidenced in the community center notice, the disease model has been established as dogma in many clinical and public health settings over the past twenty years. I think there are three primary drivers of this acceptance. First, research has shown structural and functional changes in the brains of persons with addiction. If it is assumed that something that causes structural changes to the brain is best understood as a disease and that behaviors resulting from those structural changes are involuntary, then it follows that addictive behaviors are involuntary and are best described in the language of disease. Second, the disease model is attractive because it purports to speak compassionately and non-judgmentally about persons with addiction. It therefore offers a way of avoiding some of the problems of the choice model. Third, it is instinctively attractive for medical professionals to understand problems in medical terms. Arguments that compare addiction to diabetes, for example, are instinctively appealing because they make a mystifying problem seem understandable. They seem to move a bewildering and heart-rending problem onto ground that we can control.

If addiction is a disease, however, what kind of disease is it? What syndrome does it produce? Let us consider Jayden again. When he started using opioids again, he stole electronics from his father and sold them online. He texted his dealer and arranged a meeting time and place. He purchased drugs from this person, then prepared them in specific, even ritualized, ways. He injected fentanyl into the tiny, spidery veins of his lower leg, which is not easy to do. All these actions seem goal-oriented, purposive, and willful. The disease model suggests that they are not, that our intuitive sense of some degree of willfulness is misleading. According to the disease model, Jayden's will is not involved in these behaviors. Rather, he is a passive victim of pathology. There is, therefore, no significant difference between Jayden's condition and coronary artery disease or pancreatitis in terms of how the condition relates to the will of the affected person.

The disease model claims that acts that appear to be voluntary are not voluntary; human behaviors that appear to be autonomous choices are not autonomous choices. Addiction is a disease that produces actions without choice or agency. As such, recovery does not, and cannot, arise from the will. It requires medical treatment and interventions aimed at external factors. Proponents of the disease model see this claim as humanizing and hopeful. If addiction is a medical problem, then therapeutic advances are all we need to cure it. If addiction is a medical problem, then there is hope. As Dr. Matthew Torrington, an addictions physician, once declared: "With the scientific advances we're making in understanding how the human brain works, there's no reason we can't eradicate addiction in the next 20 or 30 years. We can do it by fixing the part of the brain that turns on you during drug addiction.... I think addiction is the most beatable of all the major problems we face. And I think we will."[2] Dr. Torrington's words were published in 1995.

What's Wrong with the Disease Model?

In the years since Dr. Torrington made this statement, the addictions crisis has worsened beyond what any of us could have imagined. This failure of prediction is, of course, not just a failure of the disease model of addiction. Much has changed since 1995, mostly related to the availability of drugs, pornography, and gambling, that would have been difficult for Dr. Torrington to foresee. But the dramatic worsening of the problem, despite medical advances and widespread acceptance of treatment strategies based on the disease model, should prompt careful examination of the model's potential weaknesses. In my assessment, the disease model lacks explanatory power, most notably when considering the phenomenon of recovery. Furthermore, although proponents of the disease model are usually strongly motivated by a desire to speak about people with addiction in ways that are humanizing and compassionate,

---

2. Quoted in Denizet-Lewis, "Anti-Addiction Pill?"

some of its features undermine these good intentions. As such, it is insufficiently respectful of the human person.

Explanatory Power

As mentioned earlier, widespread acceptance of the disease model of addiction has been driven by scientific advances showing neurobiological changes in the brains of persons with addiction. The argument goes like this: *if addiction is associated with changes to brain structure and function, then it must be a disease. If addiction is associated with changes to brain structure and function, then addictive behaviors arise from a pathophysiological process and are no more related to the will of the person than the processes of any other disease.* It is as simple as that, right?

The hole in this argument is that, as addictions researcher Neil Levy says, "there are neural changes associated with and causally involved in *all* behaviors."[3] We would be very hesitant to describe all human behaviors in the language of disease. For example, we know that experienced surgeons have demonstrable changes in brain structure and function when compared to novices.[4] But no one would infer from this neuroscientific data that being an expert surgeon is pathological or that performing surgery becomes involuntary because of associated brain changes.

To generalize, a human behavior is not necessarily involuntary or pathological because it can be associated with structural changes in the brain. One might just as logically say that structural changes result *from* the exertion of will or agency, as with the expert surgeon who spent years honing her craft. There is certainly correlation between the phenomenon we call addiction and certain changes in the brain. We do have much to learn from these correlations. But a primary explanatory failure of the disease model is simply that of mistaking correlation for causation.

---

3. Levy, "Addiction Is Not a Brain Disease (and It Matters)," 1. Emphasis is Levy's.

4. See Modi et al., "Decade of Imaging Surgeons' Brain Function."

To put it simply, a human mind is not the same kind of thing as a pancreas. To accept a model that leans heavily on these kinds of comparisons is to overlook large parts of the affected person: their agency, capacity for reason, conscience, pursuit of the good, and particular social and cultural history. As Maté notes:

> On the physiological level drug addiction is a matter of brain chemistry gone askew . . . . But we cannot reduce human beings to their neurochemistry; and even if we could, people's brain physiology doesn't develop separately from their life events and their emotions. The addicts sense this. Easy as it would be to pin responsibility . . . on a chemical phenomenon, few of them do so. Few of them accept a narrow medical model of addiction as illness.[5]

The story of addiction is always more complex than a deterministic account suggests. In its suggestion that addiction is merely a brain disease, rather than a whole-person phenomenon, the disease model misses several necessary pieces of the explanatory puzzle.

This explanatory weakness has significant implications, most notably with what it suggests about the phenomenon of recovery. The disease model's foundational claim—that addiction is a medical condition that produces compulsive acts without choice—is necessarily also a claim that a person with addiction cannot choose to abstain. This implication runs against a large body of evidence indicating that many persons with addiction do recover.[6] Furthermore, many people who recover do so outside of medical models of care.

Respect for Persons

The disease model's failure to explain the phenomenon of recovery is not just a failure of explanatory power. It is a failure to have a high enough view of the human person. Jayden quit using fentanyl

---

5. Maté, *In the Realm of Hungry Ghosts*, 29.

6. See Klingemann et al., "Continuities and Changes in Self-Change Research."

3. THE DISEASE MODEL

for almost a year. He says he did so because of a promise he made to his mother. He did so without any medical treatments. The disease model can only account for this by saying he had "spontaneous temporary remission of disease." Such an interpretation is missing what is most important to respecting Jayden as a person: his particular story, unique relationships, and inspiring capacity for love, loyalty, and perseverance. The disease model only saves us from the judgmental implications of the choice model—that Jayden is a bad or incompetent agent—by suggesting that he is not an agent at all. It does not help us look across at him as a neighbor or compel us to look up at him when he displays remarkable courage, determination, and love. Christians should therefore seek an understanding of addiction that suggests a higher view of Jayden than is suggested by the disease model.

In this sense, the disease model of addiction is marked by a sad irony. I know many wonderful people who are staunchly committed to it. Their attachment to this model is usually driven by deep care for those with severe addictions and moral outrage at those who would neglect or undervalue these persons. These colleagues are desperate to avoid "othering" persons with addiction and they are rightly angry about the ways that the choice model can do this. But, in their well-motivated attempt to move away from the choice model, many have accepted a model that places *more* distance between themselves and "the other." The disease model does so by suggesting that persons with addiction have a chronic agency-destroying brain disease that places their actions outside of our ability to relate to or empathize with them. In short, it is laden with the depersonalizing implications that come with any form of determinism. It therefore cannot do the good intellectual work that most of its adherents hope for.

These weaknesses of the disease model have real-world impact on how we approach and care for those with addiction. For example, I recently cared for a patient who had been addicted to cocaine for more than ten years. She sought addictions care in medical settings many times in the past. When I saw her, she used the words "rock bottom." That week, she lost her home due to her addiction. I saw her just after four a.m. under the harsh fluorescent lights. I was tired and I felt the utter inadequacy of my own words. But I tried to talk about hope. I told her I believed that, with good help, she could rediscover a life of joy and purpose. I told her that, with good help, she could stop. Then a critically ill patient arrived in the department, and I was paged away. When I returned, she was gone. Days later, she returned to the emergency department to see me. She was on her way to a treatment facility. "Thank you for telling me that I could choose to stop," she said. "No one had ever told me that before." A strictly applied disease model would suggest that my advice was incorrect, unscientific, and perhaps even inappropriate. But as she would tell it, asserting her agency was part, although not all, of offering her whole-person care. In her case, I'm so grateful that it made a difference.

A further real-world consequence of the disease model is the way that it can isolate addicted persons by sidelining communities that should be key players in the process of recovery. A growing body of evidence affirms that communities of grace, love, and purpose are a key part of healing addiction. When addiction is understood narrowly as a disease, these communities are often seen as superfluous. If addiction is not significantly different than diabetes and solutions are to be found in medical spaces, then little effort is expended to build bridges between medical care spaces and the cultural or religious communities that should play a critical role in providing whole-person care.

In this respect, seeing addiction as a narrow medical problem is bad for everyone. It is bad for medical professionals because, in my experience, we recognize that our models of care are not enough to produce healing on their own. We know our inadequacies because we see them every day. We need help, partners in healing to wrap whole-person care around those who need it. The disease model obscures our ability to recognize communities like the church as such partners. Furthermore, widespread acceptance of the disease model inhibits the church's ability to recognize itself as a context that can produce recovery for persons with addiction. In my experience, most Christian communities want to be places of healing and recovery. However, they often struggle to know how to do so, partially because they are told that addiction is a medical problem. Most importantly, such a situation is bad for persons with addiction themselves. They need whole-person care that takes into account their medical needs but is also attentive to their story, social location, unique giftings, emotional life, and spiritual needs.

To summarize, the disease model of addiction is conceptually simple. It suggests that addictive behaviors can be adequately explained without reference to the individual's will or agency. It rightly wants to resist the choice model's implication that people with addiction are bad actors, but it suggests an alternative where people with addiction are not actors at all. Despite the good intentions of those who hold this view, it also risks dehumanization by implying that people with addiction lack will and volitional freedom. It sees them as passive victims, rather than as resilient, active persons. What we need is a view that celebrates people with addiction as potential good actors, whose deepest desires and rational minds are good gifts from God. Furthermore, we need an explanatory model that incorporates the histories and particular circumstances of people with addiction, rather than seeing these factors as non-contributory and irrelevant. Finally, we need an explanatory model that explains how people with addiction are relatable. They are not fundamentally different as persons than other human beings.

What Can We Learn from the Disease Model?

As alluded to previously, the first thing that continually strikes me about the disease-model advocates I know is that they are strongly motivated by the desire to care for and respect persons with addiction. Another notable feature of these friends and colleagues is their passion for arguments that compare addiction to diabetes or heart disease. These analogies break down in several places. Most simply, addiction is unlike these other phenomena in its effect: coronary artery disease does not act on the human mind to produce compulsive behavior contrary to the person's deeper desires.

But, if narrowly applied, these types of analogical arguments can be helpful in illustrating how we should approach persons with addiction. Addiction *is* like coronary artery disease or diabetes insofar as addiction has multifactorial causality. Furthermore, like in these diseases, the primary role of caregiving communities is not to adjudicate culpability but rather to help the other as a person deserving of respect and care. To illustrate these points, and to make my disease-model friends feel welcome, we will consider these themes by comparing addiction to heart attacks.

Multifactorial Causality

As you might expect for an emergency physician, I frequently care for patients who come to the hospital with heart attacks. In medicine we call heart attacks "acute coronary syndromes," both because we like fancy names and because heart attacks occur when the spaghetti-thin coronary arteries get blocked, resulting in loss of blood flow to the heart muscle. We know from decades of research that there are many significant risk factors for the development of an acute coronary syndrome. Some of these risk factors—genetics, anatomical variations, environmental factors, and coexisting medical conditions—do not relate to the affected person's will. Some risk factors—smoking, exercise, and diet—do relate to the will of the person to one degree or another. But, when I care for a patient with a heart attack, it is not my role to adjudicate how culpable they are for their condition. No one would suggest that I pronounce, "You are twenty percent responsible" to one heart-attack patient and "You are ninety percent responsible" to the next. Such a judgment would be unhelpful, even bizarre, for at least three reasons. First, because it is impossible to adjudicate culpability in such a complex situation. Further, such a judgment would not affect their acute medical care. And third, because such an attempt would be judgmental, positioning me in a way that would hinder the development of trust between me and my patient.

Rather, it is my job to care for the patient in a way that promotes their health. My ability to perform this role effectively is

3. THE DISEASE MODEL

strengthened when I take a non-judgmental and trust-building stance. It is helpful to know about causative factors insofar as understanding the patient's particular story may help to promote future-oriented risk reduction. It is right for me to ask my heart attack patient if he smokes, so I can encourage him to stop as a way to reduce his risk of future heart attacks. But I should do so without making absolute judgments about his culpability.

In this narrow sense, addiction *is* like acute coronary syndromes and many other diseases. We know that there are complex factors related to genetics, mental health diagnoses, social and cultural realities, and adverse childhood events that make people more likely to develop certain addictions. These factors usually do not involve the will of the affected individual. We also know that many of the factors that lead to addiction do involve the will of the affected person. Close consideration of all these factors is deeply relevant insofar as understanding them can promote healing and recovery. In my experience, considering why the person developed addiction is a necessary part of whole-person care and can promote respect and compassion. To give the disease model the most charitable reading is to understand the ways it can provide nuance to this complex conversation and suggest how we can examine causative factors without participating in impossible and unhelpful judgments about the person with addiction.

Culpability

A primary problem with the choice model is that rooting addiction in the will can seem to imply that we are less responsible to help people with severe addictions. The assumption is that we should help people based on how culpable they are for their condition. If they made their own bed, they can lie in it. On the other hand, if they are a victim, then we must help them. This framework seems to imply that care should be proportionate to moral culpability.

From a Christian perspective, however, this premise is morally unacceptable because Christ died for us while we were still his enemies. "Do not judge, so that you may not be judged," he tells us. "For the judgment you give will be the judgment you get, and the measure you give will be the measure you get. Why do you see the speck in your neighbor's eye but do not notice the log in our own eye?"[7] The speck, in this case, is the ways that a person's choices may produce and perpetuate addiction. The log, in this case, is the prideful presumption to stand above them making culpability judgments, adjudicating their worthiness of our help rather than sitting beside them on the floor. We cannot work to remove the speck until we first remove the log.

In this sense, Christians have much to learn from the moral instincts that drive the disease model: the desire to avoid a judgmental approach in favor of a compassionate one. To give the disease model a charitable reading is to see it as a helpful step toward a more humanizing and respectful approach, strongly asserting that we do have a responsibility to care for and help those with addiction. Like with the heart attack patient, our stance should be one of care and help, regardless of causative factors. In this regard, the disease model can help us move beyond a judgmental stance and point us toward the responsibility of communities to love and care for those with addiction.

Despite this helpful step, the disease model does not go far enough in its attempt to distance itself from the choice model. The disease model actually accepts the same premise, that care should be proportional to moral culpability. The difference is that, motivated by a primary desire to care, the disease model dogmatically insists on the non-culpability of every person with addiction. The psychiatrist Dalrymple writes:

> In a post-religious, specifically post-Christian world, to say of someone that he is largely, or even to a significant extent, the author of his own misfortune is to be thought to be withdrawing all sympathy from him, and to be more or less telling him that he deserves whatever he gets. He is blameworthy and nothing but blameworthy. Therefore, if compassion is to be extended to him, it has to be pretended that his own conduct or choices have

---

7. Matt 7:1–3.

3. THE DISEASE MODEL

nothing to do with his misfortune, and that no question of morality enters into the situation.[8]

Both the choice and disease models accept the premise that responsibility to care should be proportional to personal culpability. In this sense, and despite the ways that the two models are the "poles" in an increasingly polarized conversation, their deepest problems lie in the ways that they are too similar. Neither of them takes Jesus's teaching seriously enough. The Christian is set free to be cheerfully agnostic about culpability questions. We know that we are all frail, all broken, and all equally in need of grace and mercy. The Gospel liberates us to love our neighbor, not after some judgment of worthiness, but simply because each of our neighbors is God's beloved creature.

To summarize, a core question at the heart of the debates about addiction is "To what degree are people with addiction culpable for their addiction?" Choice-model advocates, seeking to be compassionate, commonly argue that people with addiction are fully culpable. Compelling them to understand this is the best way to promote agency, a critical key to recovery. Disease-model advocates, also seeking to be compassionate, commonly argue that people with addiction are not at all culpable. Compelling society to understand this is the best way to combat stigma and promote care, critical keys to supporting recovery. Both models share the premise that care should be proportional to moral culpability.

For Christians, the culpability-care premise should be recognized as immoral. We should be sufficiently compelled to care deeply for those with addiction by the truth that they are human persons. Individual choices may have contributed to the development of addiction to varying degrees, but that should not change how we treat our neighbors. We can encourage agency *and* combat harmful stigmatization of persons by engaging humbly and creatively to promote relationships of mutual trust and learning. We should care deeply about people with addictions, not because they are passive victims robbed of volition and agency, but because they

---

8. Dalrymple, "Stigma and Sympathy."

deserve our respect and are inherently valuable. A necessary part of this care is the attention of our minds, engaging the challenging task of describing addiction in more precise and humanizing ways than the choice or disease models can offer. The next chapters will consider how the resources of philosophy, Scripture, and Christian communities can produce and steward such an account.

4. A Personal Model: Addiction as (Dis)Ordering Principle

SO HOW DO WE make sense of Jayden's question: "I hate down . . . why can't I stop?" If his addiction is not a choice or a disease, then what is it? It would be tempting to try to present a third way as if it were an equally simple model. But there is a pitfall here. A superficial strength of both disease and choice models is their simplicity. In saying that the will is either everything or nothing, they make clear and easily understandable claims. But this superficial strength is a deep weakness. The simplicity of these models leads to imprecision and inadequate respect for persons.

The next two chapters draw from enduring conversations in philosophy and theology to propose a more nuanced model of addiction. I will refer to this model as the "personal model" of addiction, because it springs from the core contention that addiction is a whole-person phenomenon. It affects and is related to all aspects of the person: body, mind, and spirit. Its origins and impacts cannot be reduced to a defect in will, genes, or autonomous brain. Careful attention to key theological and philosophical themes that are common to all human persons—the ordering of loves and incontinent behavior—allows a personal lens to shed light on the conceptually complex middle ground between pure choice and irresistible compulsion. Considering these themes will help produce a nuanced definition of addiction that avoids the pitfalls of the choice and disease models while preserving the five constructive features of these models that were considered in chapters 2 and 3:

1. *Persons with addiction remain moral agents.* Recovery necessarily involves empowering a person's agency rather than denying it.
2. *Persons with addiction are relatable.* Leaning into our ability to relate to them, even when their actions seem bizarre, is a way of promoting mutual relationships of learning and growth.
3. *Addiction is a way of looking, however fruitlessly, for real goods.* Addicted persons often seek goods such as love, community, meaning, peace, courage, affection, beauty, belonging, adventure, intimacy, or purpose via addictive behaviors.
4. *Addiction is usually a phenomenon with multifactorial causality.* Examining why a person has an addiction within relationships of trust is usually a necessary step in promoting recovery.
5. *Our care for persons should not be dependent on culpability judgments.* People are variably culpable for the development of their addictions. A nuanced model will see the question of culpability as irrelevant to our responsibility to care for those with addiction.

In addition, I believe that a personal model of addiction can empower communities to be places of healing and recovery from addiction.

Defining the Personal Model

Addiction, as framed by a personal model, is characterized by the ordering of significant aspects of a person's life around a particular compulsive behavior that is contrary to the good for that person. The behavior persists, despite the person's attempts to order their life otherwise. Addiction is thus an entrapping counter-rational pressure that undermines a person's ability to meaningfully pursue the things that *really* matter the most to them. Addiction is necessarily opposed to the good because it ultimately does not deliver the good things people seek through it, and because it eclipses other goods in their lives. As such, the opposite of addiction is not simply "remission." Recovery is the process of displacing addiction with truly fruitful ways of seeking what is good.

In order to further develop a personal model of addiction, the remainder of this chapter will consider the theme of order. Addiction is an outworking of the common human need to order and structure our lives. Addiction is powerful because it provides persons with ways of "ordering" real goods. Addiction is harmful because the addictive behavior cannot ultimately produce these goods and because it erodes the person's ability to seek them in more fruitful places. The subsequent chapter will consider how the mediating category of *incontinent action* can explain addictive behavior more convincingly than the categories of pure choice and pathological compulsion that are suggested by the simpler models. Traversing this more conceptual terrain will allow us to land on practical and hopeful conclusions about how to promote freedom for our friends, neighbors, and patients who suffer from addiction.

Addiction as (Dis)Ordering Principle

Everybody craves. Everyone experiences compulsions. All persons have longings and drives that arise from someplace deeper, more difficult to control or name, than our wills. Everyone seeks, consciously or unconsciously, to satisfy deep common needs for belonging, closeness, peace, friendship, and freedom. Professor and philosopher James Smith likens human persons to "existential sharks": "To be human is to be *for* something, directed toward something, oriented toward something. To be human is to be on the move, pursuing something, *after* something. We are like existential sharks: we have to move to live. We are not just static containers for ideas; we are dynamic creatures directed toward some *end*.... To be human is to be animated and oriented by some vision of the good life."[1]

For Christians, these realities are not embarrassing or lamentable. Rather, they are evidence of our created nature as persons who were made for friendship with the God who can satisfy our deepest needs. No theologian has seen this more clearly than Saint Augustine, who famously wrote: "You have made us for yourself, O Lord, and our heart is restless until it rests in you."[2]

Another way of saying that everyone is for something is that everyone orders their life in terms of certain priorities, examined or unexamined. Smith, who is an insightful contemporary guide to the thought of Augustine, explores this theme brilliantly in his book *You Are What You Love*. Smith uses shopping, "retail therapy," as an example of something that might provide an ordering principle for one's life:[3] you are feeling an absence of purpose or significance and so you seek existential relief by going to the mall to buy something. At a superficial level, you might even feel better. You have ordered your God-given human desire for purpose according to the (often unexamined) belief that your capacity to choose to consume is what gives you purpose and significance. Smith reminds us that when we look for purpose by going to the mall, we are not just consuming but also loving, worshiping.[4]

Augustine would say that retail therapy is a bad idea, but not because he was a grumpy moralist who thought that shopping is necessarily bad. The problem is not the mall, but what you look for from the mall. Retail therapy is a bad idea because *it does not work*. The existential relief it provides is fleeting and only feeds your bottomless desire for more. You will feel a craving to go back to the mall tomorrow.

The only solution for this, Augustine tells us, is to order all the goods of our lives according to the God who made us in such a

---

1. Smith, *You Are What You Love*, 8. Emphasis is Smith's.

2. Augustine, *Confessions* 1,1.5, cited in Schaff, *Nicene and Post-Nicene Fathers*.

3. See Smith, *You Are What You Love*, 27–56.

4. See Smith, *You Are What You Love*, 38–46.

4. A PERSONAL MODEL: ADDICTION AS (DIS)ORDERING PRINCIPLE

way that the divine itself is the only thing that rightly satisfies our desires. The core project of Christian-ness is the journey toward loving God first in all domains of our lives. We believe that when we do this, our other loves will fall into place. "Seek first the kingdom of God," Christ tells us, "and all these things will be given to you as well."[5] When we love God rightly, our other loves can be ordered correctly in such a way that allows them to produce goods. But when we love other things, even good things, above God, our relationship with those things becomes distorted, literally "disordered," such that they can function contrary to the good in our lives. The simplest term to describe the state of loving something above God, intentionally or unintentionally, is idolatry.

What does all of this have to do with addiction? The insights we gain from Smith can help us move beyond the shallow analyses of the choice and disease models that view addiction as either degeneracy or pathology. Like retail therapy, addiction can be a way of looking for right, good, things in ultimately fruitless places. For example, persons consistently describe the sensation of fentanyl in terms that evoke human affection. People have told me that using it feels "like a warm hug," "like someone putting their arms around you," "like someone covering you with a warm blanket when you are out in the cold," and "like a welcome." I cannot write that sentence without seeing their faces. I believe them. As long as fentanyl is the only thing in the world that offers them things that we all desperately need—meaningful welcome, comfort, and peace—I believe that they will never stop using it. Even if it betrays and kills them.

As such, any helpful model of addiction must teach us how to look attentively at the person and ask: *"What are you really wanting when you want to drink, to gamble, to escape into social media? What are you really wanting when you want to look at pornography or shoot a point of fentanyl?"* Or, to push this theme slightly further, *"How have cigarettes become an ordering principle through which you fruitlessly seek the good things that God made you for?"*

---

5. Matt 6:33.

SECTION 1: WHAT IS ADDICTION?

The personal model of addiction suggests addiction is a way of ordering the goods of one's life. In her memoir of heroin addiction, Ann Marlowe writes: "Nonusers wonder why [addicts] don't see the absurdity of arranging their whole day around their need for heroin, but they've got it the wrong way around. One reason people become [addicts] is to find some compelling way of arranging their lives."[6] Another powerful example of the way addiction can be dis-ordering comes from Jon Elster's reflection on tobacco addiction:

> Even today I vividly remember what it was like to organize my day around smoking.
> When things went well, I reached for a cigarette. When things went badly, I did the same. I smoked before breakfast, after a meal, when I had a drink, before doing something difficult, and after doing something difficult. I always had an excuse for smoking. Smoking became a ritual that served to highlight salient aspects of experience and to impose structure on what would otherwise have been a confusing morass of events. Smoking provided the commas, semicolons, question marks, exclamation marks, and full stops of experience. It helped me achieve a feeling of mastery, a feeling that I was in charge of events rather than submitting to them. The craving for cigarettes amounts to a desire for order ... not for nicotine.[7]

To read Marlowe and Elster through the lens of theology is to see their addictions as examples of highest loves, ordering principles, and even worship. The thing one is addicted to is an idol that has entrapped a person in a cycle of ordering their life according to itself, rather than according to the God who loves them. It is evil, opposed to the good, because it does not ultimately deliver the goods that it promises. It does not work. Furthermore, it grows in their life such that there is little room for anything else. We might see a kind of tragic inversion of C. S. Lewis's famous line: "I believe in Christianity as I believe that the sun has risen: not only

---

6. Marlowe, *How to Stop Time*, 57.
7. Elster, *Strong Feelings*, 64.

because I see it, but because by it I see everything else."[8] Elster's quote could be paraphrased as: "I smoke, not as an experience among other experiences, but as something through which I experience everything else."

In short, addiction provides persons with an ordering principle for significant aspects of their lives. This lens can help us understand why addiction is so common in individualist, relativist societies. People who do not exist within thick social and moral spaces that provide meaning and belonging are more likely to seek these goods in other, potentially destructive, places. Furthermore, the theme of order can help us understand how addictions are relatable, even to those who do not share the same patterns of behavior. Addictions are ways of looking for things that we all want and need.

This theme of addiction as disordering principle also suggests helpful nuancing to the language of disease. The term "disease" in our context cannot escape the determinist implications that we have considered in prior chapters. If we accept that addiction provides an ordering principle to one's life, then it is more precise to describe addiction as a disorder rather than a disease. The term "disorder" is also more personalizing because it suggests relatability. The language of disease suggests that addiction is a problem that some people have and others do not, but the language of disorder indicates how addiction is one form of something that everyone experiences: disordered love. It is worth emphasizing again that we can say all of this without suggesting any particular culpability judgments.

Reorder and Recovery

Understanding addiction as a disordering principle has powerful implications for how we understand recovery. The implication of the disease model is that addiction is an abnormal state that can be replaced by its absence. The opposite of pneumonia

---

8. Lewis, *They Asked for a Paper*, 165.

is a non-pneumonia lung. The opposite of acute pancreatitis is a non-acute-pancreatitis pancreas. Disease language can imply that healing addiction is simply a matter of medical and basic social interventions, rather than a whole-person project that involves the total re-ordering of one's life. I work with many well-meaning people who speak as if the opposite of a fentanyl addiction is a methadone prescription and a room in a housing facility far away from the Downtown Eastside. Understanding the disordering nature of addiction can help us see why such an approach is unlikely to work. Methadone prescriptions and subsidized housing are generally good things in themselves. However, when used in isolation, they are likely to produce a *loss of meaning* in the life of a person for whom fentanyl use and the social context of the Downtown Eastside provide belonging, community, and purpose. "When I stopped getting high," Marlowe says, "what bothered me most was my relapse into loneliness."[9] It is deeply unsurprising, if of course tragic, that most people who feel this way end up back in a cycle of addictive behavior.

Journalist Johann Hari once gave a famous lecture about addiction (currently viewed over twenty-two million times) which concludes with this contention, "The opposite of addiction is not recovery. The opposite of addiction is connection."[10] This quote points to something true about addiction: it cannot be replaced with a vacuum. Furthermore, true recovery requires connections to other persons in communities of care. Hari's contention, however, does not go far enough, because *addiction is itself a connection*. Indeed, the terrifying power of addictions lies in the way they perpetually offer connections with the good things in life, even while their negative consequences overwhelm the person. Healing is not about connection *in general*. Rather, freedom from addiction is about displacing disordered connections with ordered ones through investment in particular kinds of relationships with the natural world, other human persons, and higher realities.

---

9. Marlowe, *How to Stop Time*, 140.
10. Hari, "Everything You Think You Know About Addiction Is Wrong."

4. A PERSONAL MODEL: ADDICTION AS (DIS)ORDERING PRINCIPLE

Understanding addiction as disordering principle therefore helps us see why the most effective recovery programs revolve around immersive communities that provide purpose, new habits, and friendship. These spaces do not try to replace addiction with mere remission. Rather, they try to displace addiction with other, richer ways of seeking common human goods. "The thing that kept me sober," says one testimonial from Alcoholics Anonymous's (AA's) *Big Book*, "was the love in the room of Alcoholics Anonymous. I made some friends for the first time in my life. Real friends that cared."[11]

Furthermore, understanding addiction as an ordering principle underlines the necessity of engaging questions of worship, idolatry, and highest loves as part of any rich conversation about addiction. When the Twelve Steps compel us to "believe in a power greater than ourselves," they are not sneaking religion into addictions care without good reason, as many of AA's detractors suggest. The "higher power" steps are articulating the rich psychological insight that it is very difficult to recover from addiction unless the person gives themselves over to something else with the same intensity that they had previously given themselves over to their addiction.

Christians know that we all give ourselves over to disordered loves. We believe that Jesus is the true ordering principle that rightly aligns all the goods that we were made for. The only way for each of us to be healed is to grow in friendship with God such that disordering idols are displaced in our lives by the God who cares for us. In this fundamental sense, persons with addictions do not have an additional problem when compared to everyone else. All of us need the mercy of God, the only ordering principle that can satisfy our hearts and rightly order all the goods of our lives. The challenge that addiction presents to our churches is whether we can embody the consuming, gracious, hospitable welcome of God to each person who we encounter. We will return to this challenge in subsequent chapters.

---

11. Alcoholics Anonymous, *Big Book*, 468.

5. A Personal Model: Incontinence

WE HAVE SEEN THUS far that the power of addictions lies in their ability to offer persons real goods, things that matter to all of us. Addictions are harmful because they ultimately fail to deliver these good things and because they come with undesired consequences that erode other goods of the affected person's life. The language of betrayal is common in addictions memoirs. For example, "Alcohol ... utterly betrayed me. It didn't take all that long before the drug's most reliable effect was to ensure the alienation, despair, and emptiness that I sought to medicate."[1] A defining feature of addiction that all explanatory models seek to account for is the experience of perceiving this betrayal and yet feeling unable to change one's behavior. "I drink because I'm lonely; I'm lonely because I drink," as the saying goes. In other words, one can rationally know that stopping alcohol is the best way to find healing from loneliness, yet simultaneously continue drinking as if drinking was the best way to find that same healing. One can know that heroin is not a good ordering principle for life and still behave as if it is. Addiction, therefore, is a counter-rational pressure that undermines one's ability to connect one's rational desires to one's behavior.

I encounter examples of this reality daily at St. Paul's. I would estimate that I care for at least three patients with opioid overdoses

---

1. Grisel, *Never Enough*, 7. See also White, *Recovering*, 107.

5. A PERSONAL MODEL: INCONTINENCE

per shift. Many of these persons are in our department for overdoses at least once per week. I worry about them when I see them. Then I worry for the time that I will not see them anymore. Usually these persons are too drowsy to speak to me at first. After a few hours, they are usually more alert, no longer significantly intoxicated but not yet in withdrawal. At that time, most of these patients, if asked, report a desire to stop using opioids and enter recovery. In my experience, they almost-universally say that they are desperate for freedom from addiction. However, if these patients stay in the department long enough to enter withdrawal, things usually change. They begin to indicate an overwhelming urge to acquire opioids, no matter the cost. They frequently leave the hospital mid-treatment, even in extremely medically high-risk situations. In these cases, addiction has interfered with the ability of persons to pursue the things that matter most to them. This phenomenon, where addiction undermines and entraps the person in a cycle of compulsive behavior, is perhaps most powerfully described in David Foster Wallace's *Infinite Jest*:

> Now you hate the Substance, hate it, but you still find yourself unable to stop doing it, the Substance, you find you finally want to stop more than anything on earth and it's no fun doing it anymore and you can't believe you ever liked doing it but you still can't stop . . . it's like there's two yous; and when you'd sell your own dead Mum to stop and still, you find, you can't stop . . . then you're in serious trouble, very serious trouble, and you know it, finally, a deadly serious trouble, because this Substance you thought was your one true friend, that you gave up all for, gladly . . . has finally removed its smily-face mask to reveal centerless eyes and a ravening maw . . . . You see now that It's your enemy and your worst personal nightmare and the trouble It's gotten you into is undeniable and you still can't stop.[2]

How can we account for this, for the way that addiction undermines a person's ability to act out of their rational desire

---

2. Wallace, *Infinite Jest*, 346–47.

for recovery and freedom? Neither the choice model nor the disease model can make sense of such a situation in a way that is adequately respectful of the person at the heart of it. To do so, we need a mediating philosophical category—between simple determinism and simple voluntarism—that can allow us to see how someone might truly *know* the good and yet be undermined in their ability to pursue it. I believe that the behavioral category of *incontinence*, first introduced by Aristotle, can do so in a way that is both precise and respectful of persons.

I first encountered incontinence in Dunnington's insightful book, *Addiction and Virtue*. It was initially difficult for me to see how powerful this idea was in terms of explaining addictive behavior. Admittedly, it also took me some time to get over my medically habituated association of the term "incontinence" with the word "urinary." I have, however, come to see this as an indispensable category which illuminates features of addictive behavior that are otherwise very difficult to explain. Considering Aristotle's framework may initially seem abstractly theoretical. But I have found it to be practically helpful. For example, it helped me understand and connect with Jayden. It helped me to do what a doctor should do: effectively promote his health. I believe that taking the time to understand incontinence will reveal fruitful ways of loving our neighbors with addiction. So, what is incontinence, and how does it apply to addiction?

Outlining Incontinence

In his classic ethics treatise *Nicomachean Ethics*, Aristotle outlines four categories of human action: virtuous, continent, incontinent, and vicious.[3] He also discusses an additional "morbid" category which falls outside of the realm of human behavior.[4] Although there is considerable nuance to Aristotle's thought, his schema can be helpfully summarized in the following table:

3. Aristotle, *Nicomachean Ethics*.
4. Aristotle, *Nicomachean Ethics*.

5. A PERSONAL MODEL: INCONTINENCE

Type of action	Rationally judges right from wrong?	Appetite in line with reason?	Acts in keeping with the good?	Relatable human action?
Virtuous	Yes	Yes	Yes	Yes
Continent	Yes	No	Yes	Yes
Incontinent	Yes	No	No	Yes
Vicious	No (does not)	Yes	No	Yes
Morbid	No (cannot)	n/a	n/a	No

Virtuous action is the type of action that is most consistent with the good. The virtuous actor's reason and desire align toward the good and so she acts in line with the good. We might say that the virtuous person acts entirely authentically because her reason and appetites are totally aligned. The virtuous person does what is right habitually, without having to exert her will to overcome a counter-rational appetite that tempts her away from the good. When the virtuous person's alarm clock goes off in the morning, she gets out of bed right away, knowing and feeling that keeping her commitment to have breakfast with her grandmother is part of what it means to live a life that is aligned with the good.

In contrast, the *continent* person experiences appetitive desire that tempts her away from what her reason tells her is good. When her alarm clock goes off, her rational mind tells her to get up, but a counter-rational desire tempts her to hit the snooze button and let her grandmother eat alone. The key feature of continence is acting correctly—consistent with the good—in this kind of situation. The continent person exerts her will to overcome desire in favor of reason. She slides her feet out from under the warm blankets and puts them down onto the cold floor. Virtuous action, doing what is right habitually, is preferable to continent action. And yet we should encourage continent action as good, because the only way to become a virtuous actor is to first be a continent actor. As a common teaching in the virtue ethics world goes: *You can only become a patient person by doing what a patient person would do without yet being a patient person.* In other words, the continent actor, who follows reason over desire and so does what is good, is well on her way to becoming virtuous.

The *incontinent* person experiences the same conflict between reason and desire as the continent person. Her reason tells her to keep her commitment to her grandmother, but a bodily appetite tells her to hit snooze. The incontinent person hits the snooze button. Incontinent action occurs when the person's ability to connect reason to action is successfully undermined by some internal interfering factor. In other words, something undercuts the person's ability to do what they *really* know they should do. Notably, the incontinent actor still knows what is good and is capable of aspiring to it.

The fourth category of human behavior, for Aristotle, is *vicious* action. For Aristotle, the term "vicious" is not intended to be derogatory. It simply describes behavior that arises from a habit or disposition away from the good. Persons may be variably culpable for such dispositions, which Aristotle calls vices. The vicious actor's reason and desire "authentically" align away from what is right, hence the person does what is wrong. The vicious actor hits the snooze button without any internal tension, incorrectly but truly believing that abandoning her grandmother in favor of a mid-morning doze is the right thing to do. The vicious act happens when the actor is capable of rationally approving of the good, but they do not do so. In contrast to this, Aristotle allows for a fifth category, morbid action, where the affected individual *cannot* rationally approve of the good. This person is beyond the bounds of relatable human behavior.

What does this classification of human action have to do with addiction? It is helpful here to return to Jayden's story one final time. Jayden said: "I want to stop more than anything. But I can't stop. Why can't I stop?" The choice model would say that Jayden is a vicious actor: able to keep his promise to his dying mother but freely choosing a different, destructive, vision of the good life. The disease model would say that Jayden is a morbid actor: suffering from a disease that renders his action outside the

5. A PERSONAL MODEL: INCONTINENCE

bounds of rationality or relatability. In contrast, *a personal model asserts that Jayden is an incontinent actor*: still clearly able to rationally approve of the good and yet experiencing something that undermines, to varying degrees at different times, his ability to connect that desire to his action. In other words, his addiction is a disordering phenomenon that acts within his person to impede his ability to pursue what he knows to be good. The philosophical category of incontinence articulates our intuitions about the competing desires within Jayden.

The category of incontinence therefore illuminates several features of addiction that other models cannot account for. First, it helps us clearly understand the way that persons with severe addiction remain moral agents whose deepest desires and rational minds are good gifts from God. Jayden *does* love his mother deeply and *does* know the significance of the promise he made to her. Despite his severe addiction, he has the capacity to discern and courageously pursue the good in admirable ways. The most important step in promoting his freedom from addiction is looking closely enough at him to see these deep desires and then to engage in such a way that empowers his own agency toward the good.

Second, the category of incontinence clarifies *how* addictive behaviors are relatable. Incontinence, a defining feature of addiction, is a broader phenomenon that all of us experience. We all know what incontinence feels like. Putting dramatic examples aside, it slips into our lives in small, everyday ways. For example, I can sometimes hear myself, near the end of a long night shift, being irritable with a coworker while simultaneously knowing that I should be patient. I know I am wrong, but I cannot help it. My fatigue produces incontinence. I can say, similar to Jayden: "I hate impatience, I hate it. But I can't stop myself." Identifying this similarity does not minimize the dramatic differences between myself and Jayden, but it helps me understand the ways in which we are similar. It helps me do what Maté rightly wants us to do: to recognize that I know what it feels like to have something ensnaring and oppressive "living within me" that undercuts my ability to meaningfully pursue the good. Jayden is not significantly different from me. His cry is an echo of the words of Saint Paul: "I do not understand my own actions. For I do not do what I want, but I do the very thing I hate.... But in fact it is no longer I who do it but sin that dwells within me."[5] All of us should relate to this. A personal model of addiction reveals these similarities, believing that leaning into them is a way of promoting mutual relationships of trust and growth between those with addiction and those who would care for them. A personal model can do so without sliding into Maté's overbroad definition of addiction. If all addiction involves incontinence, not all incontinence is addiction.

It is important, as a caveat, to see how the category of incontinence does not characterize all instances of behavior that may seem, externally, to be addictive. The first notable exception involves underlying pathology, such as severe psychotic illness, that prevents the affected person from having the capacity to bring reason to bear on the situation. These behaviors would rightly fall within Aristotle's category of morbid action. Whole-person care for these valuable persons requires us to address the underlying illness as much as we can, knowing that uncovering their rational capacity and moral agency are necessary steps in addressing any coexisting addiction they may have.

The second exception involves situations where persons genuinely believe that the behavior involved is consistent with the good. It is common for stories of addiction to begin this way, which further highlights the themes of betrayal and entrapment. This phenomenon is brilliantly portrayed in fiction in Barbara Kingsolver's Pulitzer-winning novel *Demon Copperhead*. The title character, a teenager, is initially prescribed oxycontin for an acute knee injury. He gradually becomes dependent on this opioid in order to function. He is told by trusted figures that opioids are the solution to his problems. He experiences the physiological phenomena of dependence, tolerance, and withdrawal. However, he believes that these experiences confirm his need for opioids rather than evidencing the threat they pose to him. This initial state, where we should rightly read Demon as a victim, is not best described in the language of

---

5. Rom 7:15–17.

5. A PERSONAL MODEL: INCONTINENCE

incontinence. As Demon gradually realizes that opioids have become a disordering principle in his life—that they have betrayed him—he begins to desire escape from the hold they have on him. At this point we can say, without suggesting any particular culpability judgment, that Demon's continued use of opioids becomes incontinent and therefore addictive in nature.

Applying a Personal Model

To summarize, a personal model begins by viewing addiction through the lens of descriptive categories that are experienced by all persons: action in line with an ordering principle and incontinent action. This model can avoid the pitfalls of simplistic choice and disease models while also retaining the good things that the simpler models seek to produce: assertion of agency, relatability, meaning, multifactorial causality, and care that is independent of culpability judgments. In psychological terms, the personal model suggests that addiction is better described as a disorder than as a disease. In theological terms, it suggests that addiction is a form of worship, and therefore oppressive idolatry, from which persons ought to be freed. In philosophical terms, a personal model suggests that addiction is a phenomenon that produces *incontinent* action, where an interfering factor impedes a person from pursuing what they know to be good. In social and cultural terms, it suggests that addiction is not just an individual problem but also a sign of community brokenness, where persons are dislocated from fruitful attachments and are offered or drawn to harmful attachments instead.[6] We will conclude this section by considering how this model can bring semantic clarity and helpful implications for recovery to conversations around addiction.

---

6. The language of dislocation follows Bruce Alexander's work on this subject. See, for example, Alexander, *Globalization of Addiction*.

SECTION 1: WHAT IS ADDICTION?

Semantic Clarity

The personal model of addiction can provide semantic clarity by helping us recognize which patterns of behavior are addictive and which are not. The framework that begins with disordering principle and incontinence can show us how addiction is not only present in extreme situations involving hard drugs. All of us probably have addictions, to varying degrees, in some seasons of our lives.

At the same time, the themes of disordering principle and incontinence can offer precision that prevents us from sliding into overly broad definitions of addiction. The personal model articulates the differences between addiction and other habitual behaviors. For example, a common disease-model argument involves the likening of substance addictions to the condition of type-one diabetes, where the person is physiologically dependent on insulin and develops "withdrawal" symptoms if they do not inject it. But the personal model can explain our intuition that there is something significantly different between the person with diabetes and the person with alcohol addiction. The person with diabetes uses insulin in a way that is congruent with their rational view of the good. For the person with alcohol addiction, alcohol masquerades as a solution for their deepest needs but they know that alcohol is *really* a part of the problem. For the diabetic, reason affirms that insulin *is* the solution and, as such, the practice of injecting it before eating is not incontinent action but rather a good habit.

We can similarly apply this lens to drinking coffee, a substance that can produce tolerance and withdrawal. Drinking coffee can also be an ordering habit through which people seek goods. For example, Kalyn and I enjoy a morning ritual of making coffee and sitting on our front steps with our mugs and a poetry collection. Often, when I feel scattered at the start of the day, I feel a compulsive need for a coffee and a poem to help order myself. Some would suggest this means I am addicted to coffee, but this would be an overbroad use of the term. Drinking coffee in this context is congruent with my view of the good, true, and beautiful. It does not produce tension between my reason and desire and exists "in order" underneath my higher loves for poetry, my wife, and God.

It is, however, possible to be addicted to coffee. Let us say, for example, that I gradually find myself unable to sleep after I drink any caffeine. Let us say, further, that I rationally identify that my coffee-driven insomnia is making me an inattentive father, a day-drowsy-driver, an insensitive physician, and a scattered teacher. In this case, if I try to stop consuming coffee but still find myself drinking it, I might be considered addicted. The key features are the development of incontinence and the way that the particular behavior becomes disordered such that it that eclipses higher goods in the life of the person.

We could consider many other examples. Is it possible to be addicted to work? What about running? Gummy worms? Social media? Romance novels? A personal model suggests that it is possible to be addicted to these things, although it helps us see the casual use of this term is often overbroad and misapplied. But the human potential to become addicted to a wide variety of behaviors highlights the way all of us should practice regular self-examination. Our healthy rhythms can become distorted and slide toward addiction if we are not attentive to stewarding them well. Seeking healing from disordered loves is not just a project for some people, it is a project for all of us. The humbling and difficult journey from incontinence, through continence, to virtue is not just a necessary path for those with severe addictions. It is a common path that all Christians must walk. We will return to this important theme in section 3.

Finally, for me one outworking of the personal model is the commitment to refer to persons like Jayden as "persons with addiction," rather than as "addicts." I use this language when I teach in healthcare settings, and I have used it in this book. In a conversation where the dignity of affected individuals is so often overlooked or denigrated, it is right to use language that points to personhood. The first thing that should be said when we talk about those with addiction, regardless of circumstance, is that they are persons: God's creatures who irreducibly and irrevocably bear God's image.

Implications for Recovery

We have already seen how a personal model illuminates why a narrow medical model of care is limited in its ability to produce recovery. To put it as simply as possible: in seeing addiction as a brain disease, medical models miss most of the person. They are tempted to view a complex whole-person experience as a mechanical or technical problem to be fixed. As a result, they try to replace addiction with "remission," a state which will often feel meaningless to the affected person for whom addiction provided a way of seeking goods, however fruitlessly.

A personal model also helps us see why forced treatment is unlikely to be effective. Recovery is not simply about imposing different superficial rhythms; it requires a whole-person re-orientation toward new ways of ordering one's life, seeking the good, and dealing with the things that tempt toward incontinence. Such a reorientation is impossible without the affected person's agency being engaged and without trusted communities of friendship that promote and develop their agency. Coercion in treatment can undercut both the meaningful engagement of the person and the development of mutually trusting relationships.

In addition to helping us see why narrow medical and coercive approaches are unlikely to be effective, a personal model can also help outline the kind of spaces that will more successfully help persons find freedom from addiction. Recovery is a whole person phenomenon that requires whole-person care. Recovery is best promoted within immersive communities that provide individuals with ways of replacing disordered rhythms with more fruitful ways of seeking the good. Furthermore, communities can promote healing by helping persons develop their agency so as to move from incontinence toward virtue.

Finally, a personal model suggests that, despite the overwhelming nature of the addiction crisis of our time, there is

5. A PERSONAL MODEL: INCONTINENCE

meaningful hope. Addiction is not a problem of hopeless degeneracy or permanent psychopathology. It is a problem that can be, and often is, healed through a cooperative effort between the agency of the person, the love of gracious communities, and the virtue-infusing work of the Holy Spirit. One of the most moving blessings that my vocation offers me is the opportunity to meet persons who have recovered from severe addictions through such a process. They are my heroes. Most of them have had moments in their story that tempted them toward accepting a hopeless view of their addiction. They are often marked by the scars left by their addiction. But, like the scars on the palms of Christ, the healed wounds on these persons are testaments to the power of God to rescue. We need to read the Bible alongside these remarkable sisters and brothers, who are learning to hunger and thirst for righteousness as they once craved alcohol or pornography. Our church communities need the blessing of the presence of these friends, from whom we can learn what it means to be totally given over to something. A personal model of addiction is necessary most basically because it helps us see these simple, personal truths. There is hope.

Section 2: **Addiction and the Bible**

The Wedding at Cana

Last night, a man came into St. Paul's because he had zipped the skin of his penis into his zipper. He was drunk. He had been in the middle of telling a story and had tried to wrap up his pee a bit too quickly so he could get back to it.

He was writhing in pain in the waiting room. His wife was sitting beside him laughing. They walked in together: him swearing and puffing, her teasing and guffawing. She was drunk too.

It was really stuck. I cut off most of his pants and injected some local anesthetic. Suddenly, he could not feel a thing and really began to enjoy himself. We had him in an area of the department where there are no separate rooms, just stretchers separated by curtains. I left for a few minutes to gather some gear. When I came back the curtains were open and two other patients were peeking through, analyzing the problem together with my patient and his wife. I tried to shoo them away, but he rebuked me.

"Let 'em stay!" he shouted, lying naked on the bed. "It'll be a great story for them, too." I told him that he might feel different about his confidentiality in a few hours and yanked the curtains shut. I started to work on the zipper, but his wife grabbed the tools out of my hand.

"This should be my job," she said matter-of-factly. "I'm his wife."

"No!" roared the patient jovially. "She castrates horses for a living. If she gets down there with tools, muscle memory will take over and she'll take the whole thing off."

"Do you really castrate horses?" I asked. She smirked and handed the tools back to me. Giggles came from the neighboring stretchers. They were a bit drunk, too, I'd guess.

I got back to work, trying to cut through the zipper slider to open things up. After a while, one of the nurses tapped in and I left to go answer a page. A few minutes later I was standing at my computer, trying to interpret a blood gas, when I was interrupted by cheering. For a few minutes there was frank jubilation because the skin on someone's penis had been freed. One of the neighbors offered his own pants to my patient as a replacement for his ruined ones. I tried to settle things down: keep the curtains closed, don't shout about penises too loudly in a shared care space.

My patient offered me a fist bump. "Come on, doc, let us have a little fun."

Bless them. Bless them.

6. Is Addiction in the Bible?

I WAS A MEDIOCRE medical student. I remember meeting with a fancy surgeon for a comprehensive evaluation of my skills after a six-week rotation. The evaluation lasted for about thirty seconds. He said: "Quentin, you are, and will always be, very average." Then he dismissed me from the room. Given my overwhelming averageness, I felt nervous when I walked into the assistant dean's office one day to ask him for an academic leave of absence. I told him I had been accepted to a master's degree program at the University of St. Andrew's in Scotland and I wanted to take time off medical school to go. He initially seemed enthusiastic. He began to talk about how he loved to hear about the special interests of medical students and was excited to hear more about mine. He pulled out a file with my name at the top of it and prepared to write a note. He asked me what I was planning on studying. I said theology. He wrote the word "theology" in tiny cursive letters under my name. He seemed less enthusiastic after that. The conversation about my interests never happened. The meeting was over a minute later.

I am grateful that my leave request was ultimately approved. I am proud that, somewhere in the bowels of the University of Alberta filing system, there lies a document that reads only: "Quentin Genuis—theology." I often reflect on that conversation, on the question the assistant dean promised but never asked: "Why do you want to study theology?"

Thinking back, my reasons had a lot to do with questions I had about the Bible. I had always known that I loved the Bible. I believed it contained answers to the deepest human questions. But the study of medicine had shown me that such answers, if they were in the Bible, were not always easy to see. I needed help knowing how to approach Scripture with the questions that my vocation compelled me to ask.

Ten years later, I frequently teach about medicine and the Bible. When I do, I often perceive others wrestling in the same way I have. This is never truer than in conversations about addiction. One of the commonest questions I am asked is: "How should we use the Bible to inform our understanding of what addiction is and how it is healed?" Most Christians have a sense that we must know how to think biblically about addiction if we want to know how to rightly engage the addictions crisis of our time. But they often struggle to know how to bring their questions about addiction to Scripture.

In my experience, Christians often want to begin by looking for a biblical term or category that is directly synonymous with the concept of addiction as we understand it. This commonly leads to the conversation starting with texts related to alcohol intoxication. "Do not get drunk with wine," Paul tells the church of Ephesus, "for that is debauchery, but be filled with the Spirit."[1] I believe that there are ways that this text might help us in our understanding of and approach to addiction. For example, Paul clearly presents a *positive* alternative to wanton drunkenness rather than simply instructing against it. Paul is not some ancient version of a "Just Say No!" campaign: commanding against something without providing a rich moral framework that helps a person see why certain choices undercut the good. Instead, Paul clearly points his fellow believers to a better way to seek the good, the true, and the beautiful. This text proclaims the good news that right relationship with God is the way to fruitfully order the goods for which we are made, including those goods we seek when we use intoxicants.

---

1. Eph 5:18.

6. IS ADDICTION IN THE BIBLE?

With that being said, I feel that the ways this text speaks to addiction are limited, most simply because intoxication and addiction are not the same phenomenon. Intoxication may be a part of the cycle of many addictions, but, as we saw in section 1, it is not the defining aspect. Not all intoxication is addiction and not all addiction is, or even involves, intoxication. As such, to try to draw a simple equivalence is potentially unhelpful and misleading, for two significant reasons.

First, accepting an intoxication-addiction equivalence is unhelpful pastorally. It can often be used to support a kind of choice model, where addiction is seen simply as a problem of recurrent, chosen, intoxication, and therefore where the solution is simply to be found in gritting one's teeth and showing more self-control.[2] Furthermore, counseling a person with alcohol addiction by telling them, "Paul says not to get drunk!" is very unlikely to be helpful, since their addiction is an entrapping phenomenon of ordering principle and incontinence. Christians should therefore seek more nuanced ways of approaching the Bible with our questions about the specific phenomenon of addiction.

Second, accepting an intoxication-addiction equivalence can tempt us toward the misleading view that the addictive object is, itself, the problem. The Bible itself strongly resists such a view. Scripture does not portray any sense that alcohol, for example, is an inherently evil substance or that its effects are necessarily dangerous. Rather, the Bible clearly depicts many ways that alcohol can be a gift to human persons.[3] This is never clearer than in Christ's first miracle of the book of John: turning water into wine to sustain the joy of a wedding reception. As one of Dostoevsky's characters muses: "Ah, that sweet miracle! It was not men's grief, but their joy Christ visited, He worked His first miracle to help men's joy ... the joy of some poor, very poor, people .... Of course they were poor, since they hadn't wine enough even at a wedding ... His heart was open even to ... simple, artless merrymaking."[4] Or, less poetically,

---

2. See, for example, Welch, "Self-Control."
3. See, for example, Ps 101:14–15; Eccl 9:7; Prov 31:6–7.
4. Dostoevsky, *Brothers Karamazov*, 310.

SECTION 2: ADDICTION AND THE BIBLE

from Mark Forsyth's *A Short History of Drunkenness*: "What matters to us is that early Christians saw wine as a Good Thing . . . Jesus providing 120 gallons of the stuff is a miracle to be celebrated. There is no suggestion that maybe the guests should all calm down a bit and have an early night. That's significant."[5]

To put it simply, the Bible does not support the notion that the root problem with alcohol addiction is alcohol, enjoyment of alcohol, or even the effects of alcohol. Alcohol is not evil, and the need for more of it to fuel human celebration is an issue worthy of the intervention of God. Similarly, the problem with fentanyl addiction is not that fentanyl itself is evil. Fentanyl can be a good gift to patients who have acute orthopedic trauma or metastatic cancer, for example. The biblical witness regarding intoxicants illuminates how the root problem of addiction is not to be found in any of the intrinsic properties of addictive objects themselves, but rather in the ways that human persons can find ourselves entrapped in destructive patterns when we use created things in disordered ways. This complexity cannot be captured by trying to draw a simple parallel between addiction and intoxication.

In absence of a simple parallel biblical category, many Christians are tempted toward a second unfruitful approach: absorbing the common secular presumption that bringing questions of addiction to the Bible is a category mistake. Most of my non-Christian friends and colleagues would consider the whole project of relating the Bible to addiction to be obviously ridiculous. They would say that our understandings of compulsive behavior have progressed, scientifically and morally, far beyond the worldview of the Bible, and therefore addiction is a category of human behavior that the Bible cannot speak to. In my experience, many Christians unconsciously share such an approach.

There is much that could be said about why I think Christians should not succumb to this second approach. Most simply, as I will show in this section, we do find texts throughout the Bible that we can rightly find to be the ground of our prayers, thoughts, words, and actions with respect to the problem of

---

5. Forsyth, *Short History of Drunkenness*, 77.

6. IS ADDICTION IN THE BIBLE?

addiction. We do not find simple unequivocal discussion of addiction or recovery in any of these passages. Neither do we find merely abstract "spiritual resources" that might successfully be applied to narrow aspects of our lives. When we take the time to listen, we find something far more important: the ground of all categories, the source of our approach to all persons, and the place where we are drawn into what is real. The Bible will seem irrelevant to addiction only until we see that it determines almost everything about how we should approach addiction.

In other words, a properly high view of the Bible is even more audacious than my non-Christian friends suspect. Our frame for this issue is not that the Bible is a narrow spiritual text that we can successfully read the real category of addiction into. Rather, the witness of the Bible is itself the real thing, through which we understand all moral and behavioral categories. The primary question is not: "how do we find ways to make the Bible apply to the problem of addiction?" Rather, we should ask: "how can we find ourselves taken up by faith into the world of Scripture, such that we see addiction and addicted persons through the eyes of the Bible?" Such an approach is incomprehensible to someone who does not seek to read the Bible from within. And yet I believe it is the correct, necessary approach.

This section seeks to unpack my conviction that Christians can see addicted persons through the eyes of the Bible in ways that are empowering and fruitful. In this chapter, we have briefly considered two ways that we cannot answer the questions of relating addiction to the world of the Bible: by finding a simply synonymous concept or by assuming that there is no relation to be found at all. The following two chapters engage two biblical passages—the parable of the father's two lost sons in Luke and the story of the Gerasene man in Mark—as examples of how we might read biblical texts as the foundation of our approach to addictions issues. Using these texts as examples will show how we might find illuminating truths about addiction through examining the witness of Scripture.

7. The Parable of the Father's Two Lost Sons

> But while he was still far off, his father saw him and was filled with compassion; he ran and put his arms around him and kissed him.[1]
>
> Now his elder son was in the field, and as he came and approached the house, he heard music and dancing.... Then he became angry and refused to go in.[2]

FOLLOWING THE WORK OF Tim Keller and others, I do not believe that "the parable of the prodigal son" is an appropriate title for the shocking and indescribably beautiful parable told by Jesus in Luke 15:11–32.[3] We will instead refer to it as "the parable of the father's two lost sons," for two primary reasons. First, because the most important thing we can say about this parable is that it is *primarily about the nature of the Father*. Although it has significant value when it reveals us to ourselves, its richest depths are plumbed when we raise our eyes to see the ways that it reveals God's prodigality: God's lavishness and reckless abandon on our behalf. Second, describing the parable as "the story of the prodigal son" can risk suggesting the very mistake the parable seeks

---

1. Luke 15:20.
2. Luke 15:25, 28.
3. See Keller, *Prodigal God*, 9–13.

7. THE PARABLE OF THE FATHER'S TWO LOST SONS

to correct: viewing the lostness of the younger brother as more significant or real than the lostness of the elder brother.

Jesus is speaking to a dual audience when he teaches the parable of the father's two lost sons: the "Pharisees and the scribes" on one hand, and the "tax collectors and sinners" on the other.[4] The former community is marked by religious piety, and the latter is visibly marked by lostness. It is not difficult to see how the brothers in the parable map onto these audiences. Two brothers, two ancient audiences. And, bringing addictions issues to this text, two kinds of contemporary communities. On one hand, "younger brother" communities that are visibly shaped by the harms of severe addictions, filled with individuals who are tempted to feel ashamed, irredeemably entrapped, and far from grace. On the other hand, "elder brother" religious communities, where people superficially seem to be in right relationship with God but can be tempted toward duplicity, pride, and self-righteousness.

We have a great deal to learn from the similarities between the sons in this parable and contemporary individuals and communities. But, before we examine the parable itself, we should note that the lines between religious communities and those marked by addiction are not as simple and clear as these comparisons could be taken to suggest. Addiction is also a common and immensely destructive problem within the church, all the more sinister because of the ways that it is often hidden. We can fruitfully consider the parallels between the brothers in the parable and present-day communities while also keeping in view this important nuancing reality.

The Younger Brother

The parable of the father's two lost sons begins with the younger brother demanding his share of his inheritance from his father. When considered in first-century context, this request is a grievous insult to the father, akin to saying "I wish you were dead." As

4. Luke 15:1–2.

Keller notes, Jesus's listeners would have been shocked by this request and would have expected the father "to respond to such a request by driving the son out of the family with nothing except physical blows."[5] Even more shockingly, the father does not do so. He instead endures the pain of insult and loss without reprisal, and lets his son leave.

The younger brother takes his newfound wealth and begins to order his life according to his own desires and cravings rather than according to relationship with the father who cares for him. Predictably, disordered living leads to suffering and entrapment. The younger brother was made for rightly ordered relationship with the father, other human persons, and the natural world. The parable clearly shows how his choice to sever right relationship with his father leads to disorder in other relationships as well. He is displaced from a just human community and, instead, finds himself impoverished in a context where "no one [gives] him anything."[6] He ends up serving animals, hungry while they have enough. Ultimately, the younger brother finds himself at a "rock bottom" place where his relationship with the father, other human persons, and the natural world have all been marred.

We should also see that the younger son is clearly presented as being fully culpable for the suffering he experiences. We might see this story as presenting a kind of "hard case" that reveals God's posture toward us *even when* we are fully at fault for harm to ourselves. As emphasized previously, we should refrain from culpability judgments when we encounter persons with addiction. But this parable reveals God's stance toward those who suffer from addiction even if they were fully culpable for the associated harms.

The younger brother comes to his senses. He leaves the distant land and begins the journey of repentance, a term that literally suggests turning around. He knows that the only real healing for him can come via reconciliation with the father who he insulted. The son has no backup plan. All he has left is to begin the journey, preparing to throw himself without reserve on the nature of the father. I can

---

5. Keller, *Prodigal God*, 22.
6. Luke 15:16.

picture him walking the long road home, stutteringly practicing his apology over and over again. I can picture him hungry, thirsty, at times doubting if he has the strength to get home at all. And it is here that the father sees him, still far off. It is here that we encounter the most important truth that this parable speaks to addiction: *The father does not allow his son to journey alone.*

The father runs—an act that would have seemed undignified to Jesus's first listeners—to embrace his lost son. The father ignores the apology, the attempts at negotiation, and immediately restores his son's position as part of the family. The nature of the father is more forgiving, more gracious, more hospitable, and more generous than the son could have ever dreamed. The younger son's story ends happily because he places faith in the nature of the father, whose power to restore is greater than the son can imagine.

Too often our hopes for those with severe addiction are too small. We are tempted to believe that there is no hope for meaningful freedom and therefore that it is enough to try to reduce the harms associated with addiction. But this parable teaches us that this is not a high enough aim. If someone had seen the younger brother alone and starving in the far-off country, would it have been enough to offer him a bit of food or help him feed the pigs for a while? Those acts would be good, but they are not enough. The only real healing for the younger son comes through reconciliation with the father via a journey of repentance. This is good news, because the father is goodness itself, mercy itself. Similarly, it is not enough for the church to work to reduce the harms of addiction. Rather, the church ought to be a place that embodies the welcome of God to those with addiction, placing faith in God's power to restore—through a cooperative effort between the individual, hospitable communities, and the work of the Holy Spirit—what may seem un-mendable to us.

If you are struggling under the heavy weight of an addiction, the parable of the father's two lost sons speaks to your situation. It proclaims the Christian truth that God's stance toward you is not one of anger or desire to punish. God cares for you. God can see you, no matter how far off you find yourself, no matter how lonely or ashamed your addiction has made you feel. Becoming incarnate in Jesus Christ, he has left his own home to meet you on the road, so that you may know that you do not have to journey alone. He has gone to any length—all lengths—to rescue you. Do not despair, for there is hope.

The Elder Brother

When considered in ancient context, the elder brother's refusal to enter his father's celebration is also a grievous insult to his father. As Keller notes, Jesus's first listeners would have been shocked by the elder brother's behavior: "In a culture where respect and deference to elders was all important, such behavior is outrageous."[7] The response of the father is even more surprising. Like with the younger brother's return, the father lowers himself by leaving his own home to try to retrieve a beloved son. He endures the pain of insult without reprisal and pleads with his elder son to come inside.

But the elder brother will not be convinced. He points to the ways that the younger brother's life has been obviously, visibly, marked by disordered loves. How could the father restore one who has done such destructive things? What the elder brother does not see is that his grievance is actually against the father, not the wayward younger brother. The elder brother does not accept the unconditionally loving, gracious nature of the father, and so is ultimately revealed to be further from right relationship with the father than the younger brother is. The story concludes with the elder brother outside the father's house, still beloved and invited, but lost.

To summarize: The younger brother's life seems dramatic and wretched. For the younger brother—imprisoned by the consequences of broken relationships and misordered loves—the only real healing is that which is found in reconciliation with the father. The younger brother's story ends happily because he

---

7. Keller, *Prodigal God*, 31.

throws himself without reserve on the father's grace. The elder brother's life seems ordered and faithful. But he also finds himself imprisoned by the self-imposed consequences of broken relationships and misordered loves. The only real healing for the older brother is that which would be found in reconciliation with the father. In contrast, his story ends tragically because he pridefully holds himself above his younger brother and therefore cannot accept the father's grace and unconditional love.

The elder brother's story should convict us. All too often, churches are places where people try to put on their best faces and where honest discussion of our deep wounds and disordered loves are tacitly discouraged. Aaron White clearly articulates a common consequence of this environment for persons with addictions: "People in recovery often feel like they must prove themselves and their worthiness to be welcomed into the church. This suspicious and inhospitable attitude from the 'older siblings' hinders the creation of kinship communities . . . . It also reveals how those inside the church need illumination about what it means to be a child of God."[8] If we want our churches to be places of grace that embody the welcome of the Father, we need to have our own souls healed of the pride and self-righteousness that so often inhibit us from loving our suffering neighbors. As long as we hold ourselves above people with severe addictions, as long as we focus only on patterns of disordered behavior and miss the significance of the person, we miss—or, worse, actively resist—the amazing ways that God's grace is at work in and through them.

If you are a Christian person who is distressed or appalled by the ways that another person's addiction causes harm, the parable of the father's two lost sons speaks to your situation. It proclaims the Gospel truth that, no matter how culpable they may be for the harms their addiction causes, that person is beloved by God and so ought to compel your respect and even your reverence. Moreover, to quote novelist Graham Greene, who himself had significant addictions, you also are entirely dependent on

---

8. White, *Recovering*, 109.

"the appalling... strangeness of the mercy of God."[9] If you hold yourself above those with addiction, refusing to believe that their restoration is possible, you are not merely disrespecting them. In missing the depth of God's grace for them, you are missing the depth of God's grace for yourself. If you want to embody God's welcome, you first need to understand God's utter gratuity toward all of us. Often, there are no better friends to help us on such a journey than the restored "younger brothers" in our communities who know what it is to be wholly dependent on the grace and power of our Heavenly Father.

Living Within the Text

In my view, this text suggests specific and practical conclusions for how Christians should think, pray, and act with respect to addiction. We should confess that each of us resembles each of the brothers in different ways at different points in our lives. Another way to say this is that all of us participate in sin: that which distorts right relationship with God, other human persons, and the natural world. We should celebrate how God, in Jesus, came to rescue sinners while we were still far off on the road or standing outside the party with our arms crossed. We should therefore expend our most devoted efforts to making our local churches places that reflect God's radical welcome. We should have disciplined hope in the power of God to rescue, even in situations of very severe addiction. We should therefore challenge approaches to addiction that seek only to reduce its harms and fail to seek meaningful freedom for the affected person. We should see how most people who seek freedom from addiction need help on the road to recovery. We should pray for the eyes of Christ to recognize these persons, for creativity that inspires relationships of mutual trust, and for humility to know our equal need for friendship and grace. Finally, we should pray for perseverance to walk faithfully, together, toward the joyful welcome that the Father has in store for us.

---

9. Greene, *Brighton Rock*, 349. Ellipsis is Greene's.

8. The Gerasene Man

> Then Jesus asked him, "What is your name?"[1]

MARK 5:1–20 DESCRIBES AN event from the life of Christ that initially seems to have nothing to do with addiction. Jesus has just traveled across the sea of Galilee to the region of Gergesa. He is met upon arrival by a man who is possessed by "unclean spirits"[2] that compel him to act in dangerous and violent ways. Jesus commands them to leave the man. After a brief negotiation, Jesus permits the unclean spirits to enter a nearby herd of pigs. The pigs drown themselves in the lake. Jesus commissions the freed man to share the good news of what has happened to him. Other inhabitants of Gergesa, apparently disturbed by these events, beg Jesus to leave. He does.

I expect that many readers are instinctively wary about considering connections between our contemporary addiction crisis and this text. I certainly was. The distance between ancient Gergesa and St. Paul's Hospital seemed impossible to cross. I was afraid that any attempt to speak from this text about addiction would be heard as drawing a simple parallel between demon possession and addiction. I believed, and continue to believe, that suggesting this simple parallel would be imprecise and misleading. But it is also possible to be too cautious. If we presume that this passage *cannot*

1. Mark 5:9.
2. Mark 5:13.

speak to our questions about addiction, we bias ourselves in ways that prevent us from doing what Christians should do: reading and receiving the text. Attempting to find ourselves within it, to inhabit it as we engage in our vocations. When we are willing to simply listen to what this strange and beautiful account from the life of Christ says, we will find that it speaks to our questions about addiction in ways that are convicting and clarifying.

The Gerasene Man and Addiction

In the Gerasene man, we meet a person in the world of the Bible of whom we can rightly say both: "it is him who is acting" and: "it is not him who is acting." In one sense, it is obviously true that it is the Gerasene man who is howling, breaking shackles, and bruising himself with stones. It is his God-given mouth that is screaming, his arms straining at shackles, and his blood pooling to form bruises. In another equally real sense, his actions come from an oppressive force that resides within his person and which interferes with his ability to act freely.

It is worth noting that, if the Gerasene man is one biblical example of this phenomenon, we have already encountered another example: Saint Paul. Romans 7 is worth reading again here: "For I do not do what I want, but I do the very thing I hate.... But in fact it is no longer I who do it but sin that dwells within me.... For the desire to do the good lies close at hand, but not the ability. For I do not do the good I want, but the evil I do not want is what I do. Now if I do what I do not want, it is no longer I who do it but sin that dwells within me."[3] Saint Paul, too, felt the ensnaring and oppressive power of something dwelling within his person and interfering with his ability to pursue the good.

Addiction is another example of such an oppressive and ensnaring force. To use the language of section 1, it is an entrapping counter-rational pressure that undermines the capacity of the person to freely pursue the things that matter most to them.

---

3. Rom 7:15b–20. For another, beautiful, example of connecting addiction to this text, see Castro, "Recovering from Heroin and Fiction."

8. THE GERASENE MAN

Addiction has the potential to be just as real and powerful in the life of the affected person as the forces that oppressed the Gerasene man, even if addiction does not possess *being* in the same sense that the unclean spirits seem to in this passage.

To summarize: the Gerasene man is a clear biblical example of a person who is afflicted by an oppressing phenomenon that undermines his voluntary control and inhibits him from pursuing the good. We can therefore see fruitful points of analogy between this man's condition and the experience of persons with addiction, even if those analogies break down in some places. Furthermore, we can also recognize that the Gerasene man is an extreme case, where the dignity and agency of the person are very difficult to recognize beneath the weight of the oppressive force that torments him. His neighbors have responded to the situation by seeing him as beyond hope and expelling him from the human community where he formerly belonged. We might say that they *stigmatize* him in the strongest possible terms. We recognize that the response of contemporary human communities to persons with severe addiction is often similar. But how does God approach such a person?

Jesus asks the Gerasene man his name. What a beautiful moment this is! The eyes of Christ recognize the person, God's beloved creature, despite the depth of his suffering and torment. The importance of this point is only further underscored when the demons answer instead of the man, revealing how utterly entrapped he is. It is notable that this is the only place in the book of Mark where Jesus asks a supplicant their name, further supporting the significance of such a question in this specific case. It is particularly fitting for Jesus to assert the personhood of the Gerasene man by asking his name because his personhood is precisely what is most obscured by the demons. Just as it is beautifully fitting for Jesus to touch the leprous man prior to healing him in Mark 1, here it is profoundly meaningful that Jesus addresses the victim as a person *before* expelling the demons. *What is your name? Who are you, really?*

It does not take any great interpretive leap to apply this text to our approach to persons with addiction. It stands, first, as a stark, convicting challenge to the church: will we go and do likewise? Will we cultivate the eyes of Christ to recognize the personhood of those with severe addictions? Will we draw close to them in friendship, close enough to know their names, close enough to assert their freedom through the power of God's Holy Spirit?

We meet the Gerasene man again later in the text. He has been freed and restored by the power of Christ's welcome. Moreover, Jesus gives him an evangelistic task, telling him to go and tell his neighbors about what Jesus has done. This is another notable exception to Jesus's usual response to supplicants in the book of Mark.[4] In what is commonly called the "Messianic Secret" motif, Jesus usually tells those who he has healed not to tell anyone. The Gerasene man, told to spread the Gospel to the gentiles, is an exception to this pattern. He is freed from oppression not just to exist as he did before, but to be a laborer in the beautiful work of the Gospel.

Here, too, it is easy to see how this text should inform our approach to those with addiction. Like Jesus, we should recognize the dignity of the person and draw close to them, believing that asserting their personhood is a powerful way to promote healing. We should have robust hope for recovery, without needing addicted persons to be "in recovery" prior to seeing them as agents in and through whom God can work. We should see the potential for persons with addiction to become powerful examples, mentors, and leaders in the church, precisely because of the ways that their particular stories can bear witness to the power of God to rescue.

Finally, we should note the response of the Gerasene community to the action of Jesus. When they hear what has happened, they beg Jesus to leave their region. They are apparently unsettled because of what must have seemed to them to be the cost of the healing of their neighbor: the loss of some pigs. For his own neighbors, the freeing of the Gerasene man from torment is not worth it, for *economic* reasons. Here, also, it is not difficult to see how this text should convict and direct us in our response to the addiction crisis of our own time. The Gerasene community ultimately did

---

4. See Genuis, "Dignity Reevaluated."

not see the freedom of their neighbor as worth the loss of financial capital for others in the community. Often our society is the same: one reason we are drawn to simple models and quick fixes is that we are unwilling to invest our time, money, and labor toward complex models and costly fixes. But the solutions to our present addiction crisis will not be fast, easy, or cheap. There is no simple government-mandated policy fix. People in your neighborhood with addiction will often require significant investment—of time, space, and money—from the other people in your neighborhood if they are to find recovery. Communities that want to mirror Christ's radical welcome to those with addiction must be willing to invest in recovery because of a counter-cultural belief in the intrinsic value and dignity of all persons. When we do so, we will find ourselves deeply blessed by the presence of new friends.

Living Within the Text

I live within this story every shift at St. Paul's. I try, feebly, to recognize and assert the personhood of each of my patients, particularly those with severe addictions. I repeat to myself, "this is a person who God loves, and who should therefore compel my respect and reverence." I try to address each patient as a neighbor with inherent personal dignity. I try to be attentive enough to see how I can offer gifts of hospitality and care. Usually, the first step in doing so is asking: "What is your name?" I try to know when to simply sit beside them in silence, offering the meagerness of my presence when their grief or suffering lies beyond words. I try to pray for freedom from entrapment through the power of the Holy Spirit. And I fail, every shift, to do enough. I am so often trapped and limited by my own bad habits, wounds, and vices. For I am also subject to ensnaring forces that undermine my pursuit of the good. I—like my patients, like Saint Paul, like the man who was legion—am entirely dependent on the God who comes close to me and asks with overwhelming gentleness: "What is your name?" Like the parable of the father's two lost sons, the story of the Gerasene man reminds us to first find ourselves in the text as the one in need of rescue. Only then can we humbly hope to be vessels through whom God works to bring freedom and healing to others.

Finding Addiction in Other Texts

These past two chapters have considered two texts from the Gospels as examples of how we might come to the Bible with our questions, hopes, fears, and prayers relating to contemporary addictions issues. Using a similar approach, we can find powerful truths relating to addiction in other passages. For examples: Israel choosing a king in 1 Sam 8, Israel's cycles of apostasy, the books of Ezra and Nehemiah, the parable of the lost sheep, and Paul's theology of sin and grace.[5] Similar to the passages we have considered here, we will not find simple unequivocal discussion of addiction in any of these texts. Neither do we find merely abstract spiritual truths. Rather, when we take the time to listen, we will discover the ways that God's story of redemption illuminates all aspects of human experience, including addiction. The Bible will seem irrelevant to addiction only until we see that it determines almost everything about how we should approach addiction. The task of connecting biblical texts to the myriad practical questions that are raised by our contemporary addictions crisis requires the life of an interpreting, worshiping community within which careful intellectual and embodied work can occur. The next section is devoted in part to the question of how the church can be such a place.

---

5. For the applicability of Pauline theology here, see, for example, Carson, "Freedom and Its Anxieties."

Section 3: **Addiction and the Life of the Church**

Every Sunday someone hands me a little cube of bread. I dip it into a cup of wine. Every Sunday, someone says to me: "The body of Christ, broken for you. The blood of Christ, shed for you." I take and eat.

I sit. Every Sunday, often unbidden, this prayer comes:

"Body of Christ, broken for those who are slumped over on orange chairs in Triage Hallway;

Blood of Christ, shed for the ones on Narcan infusions;

Body of Christ, broken for those with violence flags on their charts;

Blood of Christ, shed for the ones with fresh track marks on their arms;

Body of Christ, broken for those who are banned from the shelters;

Blood of Christ, shed for the ones with delusional parasitosis;

Body of Christ for those who hope without hope that fentanyl will make them forget;

Blood of Christ for the ones with maggots in their leg wounds;

Body of Christ for those who inject with dirty needles;

Blood of Christ for the malingerers;

Body of Christ for those with endocarditis and septic emboli;

Blood of Christ for the ones who cannot seem to stay on their meds;

Body for those who are paranoid and hallucinating.

Blood for the ones sleeping on Hastings without shoes;

Body for those in precipitated withdrawal;

Blood for the ones who cry like children when we change their bandages;

Body for those who leave against medical advice;

Blood for the ones who are certified and restrained;

Body for those brought in after a first-ever overdose;

Blood for the ones who are stretchered in after their last.

Body and Blood.

Broken and Shed."

I don't want any victory that doesn't include them.

At the cross, God damns (goddamn!) any victory that doesn't include them.

I don't want any victory that doesn't include them.

9. Refuge

> The church should—for God's sake and by the work of the Holy Spirit—be a place of refuge, hospitality, and friendship for persons with addiction.

Framing the Conversation

MY PRIMARY TEACHING SETTING these days, Emergency Medicine seminars, usually revolves around discussion of patient cases. I brought the same approach, albeit with less thoracotomies, when I was recently invited to teach a medical ethics lecture to a group of seminary students. This is one of the cases we discussed:

> The parents of a seventeen-year-old boy in your congregation ask if you will meet with their family. Over the past few months their son has begun using drugs. He has stopped attending school regularly, he disappears for several days at a time, and he steals money and electronics from their home. They recently found needles in his room. This led to a confrontation in which he admitted that he has been using drugs called "down and -cide." His parents took him to see an addictions physician, "but they just offered replacement medicines," which the son has started taking but have not resulted in any significant change to his pattern of illicit drug use. The parents have read about twelve-step programs, but they are not sure if they will be helpful. The son, who you know well, is sometimes desperate for help and sometimes seems

resistant. He has agreed to meet with you, together with his parents, for advice.

After sharing the case, I emphasized to the seminarians that this kind of situation is common. I frequently see versions of this scenario play out in the emergency department. I have encountered similar cases in my own extended family and church. If pastors are not encountering these situations, it is not because they are not happening. I asked the students what they would do if they were the minister in such a situation. The primary responses focused on support outside the church community: "I would tell them to go back and see the doctor again to request expedited access to recovery facilities"; "I would help them advocate for more health resources"; and: "I would offer to accompany them to their next visit to provide spiritual care and support." I agreed that these pieces of advice have the potential to help a family in this situation. It is right for the church to point to medical services when people have specific needs that might require medical care. It is, of course, wonderful for pastors and other Christian friends to provide support by accompanying sisters and brothers to appointments. But is that a sufficient response from the body that hopes to be the hands and feet of Christ?

As I spoke to the students in the seminar, it became clear that they saw addiction through the eyes of the disease model. They viewed the journey of recovery as primarily a medical journey. As such, they saw Christian communities as, at most, a potentially helpful adjunct to support the recovery process. They wanted to offer more to this suffering family, but tacit acceptance of a narrow medical model inhibited them from knowing how to do so.

A personal model of addiction provides a richer intellectual framework that allows us to see how communities like the church are the places that belong at the center of journeys of recovery. It also shows how, if the church wants to live into this calling, it needs to be an immersive community that is centered around a shared ordering principle, that offers refuge and opportunities to build friendships, and that helps individuals develop their own agency toward the good. This does not suggest the church as a

9. REFUGE

simple alternative to medical spaces. Rather, it suggests that a church community should hope to provide whole-person care to the members of this family while also cheerfully supporting appropriate medical care.

But how do we do so? In the final section of the book, I propose an answer that flows from the intellectual and biblical frameworks considered in prior sections. Each chapter is written around a central statement asserting what Christian communities should be doing as we move toward being places of healing and recovery. I will highlight Christian individuals and groups that are already living out of these convictions and from whom we can therefore learn. Of note, these are not tasks that can be accomplished by church leaders or formal programming alone. They are convictions about what features should characterize the Christian community, necessitating the participation of each member.

This first chapter of section 3 asserts that the church should be a place that offers refuge, hospitality, and friendship for persons with addiction. These intertwined practices are the soil that nurtures individual agency, communities of giving and receiving, and liturgical rhythms that re-order our lives under the care of God. They are necessary if we want our churches to be places of recovery from addiction. More basically, they are necessary if we want our churches to be places of discipleship and sanctification for all of us.

Refuge

There is a brightly painted mural on the outside wall of a restaurant that is about two blocks from St. Paul's Hospital. I usually pass it on my way to work. The mural depicts a portrait of the late American chef Anthony Bourdain, alongside a quote from one of his books: "Your body is not a temple, it's an amusement park. Enjoy the ride."[1] Sometimes I joke that if I ever go to jail it will be for defacing that mural. Bourdain's maxim may sound like good news to the people

---

1. Bourdain, *Kitchen Confidential*, 81.

sitting inside the restaurant drinking twenty-eight dollar cocktails. But what about those lying on the sidewalk outside who are teetering on the fine line between opioid intoxication and overdose, life and death? What about the persons for whom enjoyment is only a hazy memory, buried beneath the paranoia that comes from years of smoking amphetamines? Bourdain's quote is an outworking of a common contemporary anthropology (a view of what it is to be human) that suggests our value is linked to our autonomy: our capacity to independently choose, consume, and enjoy. This anthropology may seem appealing to those who are wealthy and able-bodied, those who mistakenly believe that they are not deeply dependent on other human persons and on the natural world. But it is a taunt to the persons lying beneath the mural in the rain. Francis Spufford reflects on the implications of glib slogans like Bourdain's: "What it means, if it's true, is that anyone who isn't enjoying themselves is entirely on their own . . . let's be clear about the emotional logic . . . . It amounts to a denial of hope or consolation, on any but the most chirpy, squeaky, bubble-gummy reading of the human situation. St Augustine called this kind of thing 'cruel optimism' fifteen hundred years ago, and it's still cruel."[2]

A refuge is a place of safety and shelter, usually in the context of a surrounding environment that is unwelcoming or dangerous. Despite many well-intentioned efforts to reduce stigmatization of persons with addiction, the church in our time exists within a societal context that is functionally unwelcoming to these persons. This has roots in widespread acceptance of explanatory models that place dehumanizing distance between ourselves and those with addictions. At a deeper level, it has a lot to do with Bourdain-mural anthropology. Prizing autonomy as the principal marker of human value necessarily suggests that those who have conditions that inhibit their ability to act freely have lesser value as persons. Moral theologian Charles Camosy has written recently about the resultant development of a "throwaway

---

2. Spufford, *Unapologetic*, 11. Spufford is referencing Richard Dawkins's famous bus advertisements that proclaimed: "There's probably no God. Now stop worrying and enjoy your life."

9. REFUGE

culture," which views some human persons as less valuable because of reduced autonomy or capacity.[3] Our society's neglect of persons with addiction is one face of this throwaway culture. All too often, we respond to those with severe addictions like the Gerasene community responded to their afflicted neighbor. We assume that they are beyond help and fail to recognize their personhood, inherent dignity, and intrinsic value. In such a context, persons with addiction need places of refuge where their equal personal dignity can be recognized and celebrated.

How can the church work to be such a place? First, by repenting of the ways that we order our own lives and faith communities according to the idol of autonomy rather than the loving care of God. To do so, we need to be willing to share our own needs, doubts, fears, wounds, and addictions. We need to narrate and structure our lives in terms of our dependence on God and on each other, not around aspirations of autonomy (literally "self-rule"). As theologian Stanley Hauerwas has written: "The last thing that the Church wants is a bunch of autonomous, free individuals. We want people who know how to express authentic need, because that creates community."[4] The church needs to have a recognizable witness of interdependence if we want other dependent persons to see our communities as places of refuge amid a societal context that equates dependence with burdensomeness. Second, we can be a place of refuge by working to develop thick social networks of what Alasdair MacIntyre calls "uncalculated giving and graceful receiving."[5] These local networks should have the capacity to offer practical daily help to those who need it: meals, companionship, laundry, etc. Third, we need to invest time and resources in developing the virtue of hospitality, to which we will now turn.

---

3. See Camosy, *Resisting Throwaway Culture*.
4. Hauerwas, "Abortion, Theologically Understood," 949.
5. MacIntyre, *Dependent Rational Animals*, 121.

SECTION 3: ADDICTION AND THE LIFE OF THE CHURCH

Hospitality

Henri Nouwen describes hospitality as "the creation of a free space where the stranger can enter and become a friend instead of an enemy. Hospitality is not to change people, but to offer them space where change can take place."[6] He further describes hospitality as creating emptiness, "not a fearful emptiness, but a friendly emptiness where strangers can enter and discover themselves as created free."[7] Christian hospitality, this practice of making space for other persons, most obviously references the cultivation of welcoming physical spaces. But Christians should not restrict themselves to thinking only of church basements, community centers, shelters, or recovery facilities. If Christian communities are to be places of refuge and recovery for persons with addiction, we need to begin by making space at our own kitchen tables, on our living room couches, and in our spare bedrooms.

Churches should also invest in creating and cultivating larger spaces for community gatherings. Such a project can be extremely challenging, especially in densely populated and expensive cities. Nonetheless, if Christian communities want to promote healing for persons with addiction, we need to invest in such spaces. One example of this in Vancouver is a community called Jacob's Well. Members of this community gather in a "living room space" in the heart of the Downtown Eastside.[8] Participants have daily opportunities to partake in shared activities that open up space for the re-ordering of one's life around the rhythms of a community of friendship and grace. I go there once a week with my children for board games night.

The team that leads Jacob's Well is confident that members of this community have higher rates of recovery from addiction and overall better health outcomes. Participation in a shared physical space fosters the growth of a community of belonging. I think there is something critically important in these observations.

6. Nouwen, *Reaching Out*, 56.
7. Nouwen, *Reaching Out*, 56.
8. See Jacob's Well, "Our Vision and Values."

9. REFUGE

When working the night shift, I see so many patients who register in the emergency department essentially because they have no place to go. They need hospitality. I am grateful that places like Jacob's Well exist to meet these needs. Vancouver, like all our cities, desperately needs more spaces like it. Who better to invest in creating such spaces than local churches?

The virtue of hospitality also suggests creating spaces of time to talk and listen to strangers. I am sometimes asked how I think Christians should respond to strangers who are asking for help on streetcorners or intersections. First, it is important to say that we should not presume that all these individuals have addictions. The only way to know would be to come close enough to get to know them well. At minimum, Christians should always smile and greet these persons, thus recognizing their dignity and opening space for further interaction. This does not necessarily require further engagement in every instance. Sometimes we are appropriately engaged in a different task that aligns with our vocation and pursuit of the good. But if our plans are never disrupted by these interactions, if our lives never allow time to engage further with these potential friends, then we need to grow in this aspect of hospitality.

I am also frequently asked about the risks of hospitality. For example, someone recently asked me: "What are the risks of sharing spaces with people who have drug addictions?" The people who ask these questions are often apprehensive about needlestick injuries or unpredictable behavior from someone who may be intoxicated. These are real risks for those of us who work in neighborhoods like the Downtown Eastside. But the fundamental Christian answer to this question is clear: the risk to your own soul of *not* coming close to these persons is far greater than the risks of seeking friendship with them. I am not suggesting that we should be imprudent about minimizing risk. But if our first question is one of self-preservation, then we are wrongly, sinfully, misfocused. Rather, our focus should be on imitation of Christ, who reached across unfathomable distance to rescue us. I cannot say it better than Saint Paul: "Let each of you look not to your own interests, but to the interests of others. Let the same mind be in you that was in Christ Jesus, who . . . emptied himself, taking the form of a slave, assuming human likeness. And being found in appearance as a human, he humbled himself and became obedient to the point of death—even death on a cross."[9] When Paul tells us to have the same mind as Christ, he is giving us a concrete exhortation to focus not on self-preservation but to be willing to empty ourselves for the sake of others. Such self-emptying should include accepting the risks associated with the practice of hospitality. The beautiful thing about doing so is that we encounter Christ in the other when we do. Because Christ came into the world as a vulnerable stranger, we meet him in a special way when we hospitably welcome vulnerable strangers who live in our own communities.

Friendship

In addition to providing spaces of refuge and hospitality for those with addiction, Christian communities should be places of friendship. Friendships are chosen reciprocal relationships of trust, learning, and growth toward the good. Rich friendships are not simply utilitarian relationships based on shared interests or activities. Good friends are those who know and appreciate us, who direct us toward what is good, and thus care for our souls. Most of my patients with addiction report deep loneliness. They hunger for this kind of friendship. Friendship matters for the displacement of addiction.

I recently took my daughter to visit a friend, Katie, who was staying at a recovery unit. On this day, Katie was particularly excited for our visit because it meant that she could leave the unit for a cigarette break. She knew the rules: patients are not allowed to go off unit unless someone comes to take them for a walk. The nurses told me she had been restless all day, asking repeatedly when we would come so she could have a smoke. We arrived with tiramisu and talked with Katie while she ate it. She told us about how much she missed her children. We looked at pictures

---

9. Phil 2:4–5, 7–8.

9. REFUGE

of them and dreamed about a future where she was with them. Then we headed out for our walk. When we were almost at the door, one of the nurses ran up behind us. "Katie!" she was calling. "Katie, you forgot your cigarettes." Katie paused and looked at my daughter. Then she turned to the nurse. "No thanks, I don't need them anymore." Katie smiled and walked out of the door ahead of us. I do not think it is an exaggeration to say that the presence of friends replaced Katie's need for a cigarette.

If we are attentive to providing spaces of refuge and hospitality, the goods of friendship can arise surprisingly quickly. For example, I recently cared for a man who came to St. Paul's because he had a laceration on his forehead. A medical student working with me enthusiastically volunteered to stitch up the cut. When she finished, I walked over to check her work and assess the patient. The stitches looked great. The medical student had told me that she had been nervous and the patient had been kind and encouraging to her. I was grateful to him, not sure if I could have been similarly gracious if I was a patient in the emergency department in the middle of the night.

The patient was lying on a stretcher. He was wearing an oversized green sweatshirt with a large skull and the words "Till Death" screen-printed on the front. It was soaking wet. He was "on the nod," a phrase we commonly use to describe the particular drowsiness of those who are intoxicated on opioids. I asked him how he cut his forehead. He told me: "I used fentanyl tonight for the first time in six months. I must have used too much, because I went down. I cut my head on something. I woke up in a puddle and dragged myself here." I asked him if there was anything else we could do to help him. He said no. "I'm still pretty out of it, but tomorrow I'm going to be devastated. I'll just have to call my sponsor and try to start again." I asked again if there was any other way we could show care for him. He said he hated the soaked skull-emblazoned sweatshirt that he had got from a shelter. I fetched my jacket and gave it to him. We walked to the door together and stood there for a long moment. He asked if he could give me his sweater in return. I took it and thanked him. I told him I had hope for his sustained recovery and he was always welcome at St. Paul's. I told him I would think of him. We shook hands, standing there with our swapped clothes. We talked about where we grew up and how we ended up in Vancouver. And then he was gone.

I wear his sweater frequently now. I wear it as a way of praying for him, remembering what he taught me, and hoping I will see him again. I am wearing it as I write this. I believe that he and I experienced some of the goods of friendship in those precious minutes, even in the hectic environment of St. Paul's emergency department. Although valuable and a demonstration of friendship, these brief interactions are not sufficient to sustain us. All of us need longer-term friendships as part of growing toward the good, true, and beautiful. But we should nonetheless be attentive to the ways that mutual relationships can blossom in surprising places.

Bringing It All Together

We all need refuge, hospitality, and friendship. Persons with addiction are often denied these human essentials. It is therefore critical that the church devote specific attention to offering refuge, hospitality, and friendship to our neighbors with addiction.

We can promote recovery through these practices, as they empower the agency of persons and immerse them in new ways of relating to the good. If we want to recover and sustain these practices, we must invest vulnerably in communities of uncalculated giving and graceful receiving. We must grow in practical, costly hospitality. Finally, we must humbly and creatively pursue friendships with others who may seem very different from us, believing that in doing so we meet and minister to the God who came to us as a vulnerable, befriending stranger.

10. Nature

> The church should be a place where we are empowered—for God's sake and by the work of the Holy Spirit—to see and affirm the good desires that stand underneath addictive behaviors, knowing addicted persons to have a God-given nature.

What Is the Root of Addiction?

THINKERS WHO ARE UNCOMFORTABLE with simplistic models of addiction often seek nuance by framing addiction as a phenomenon that is rooted in the human experience of suffering. Gabor Maté, probably the most-cited example of this approach, writes: "addiction is neither a choice nor a disease, but *originates* in a human being's desperate attempt to solve . . . the problem of pain."[1] Further, he argues that persons with certain adverse childhood experiences are neurobiologically wired in such a way that will *necessarily* lead to addiction. A variety of other contemporary thinkers have followed a similar line of argument to assert that the first cause of addiction is suffering.[2]

This argument can be charitably viewed as a step in the right direction. Unlike the choice and disease models, it orients us toward the story of the affected person. But this argument does

---

1. Maté, "Beyond Drugs." Emphasis is mine.
2. See, for example: White, *Recovering*, 16; Smithwick, *Knocking on Freedom's Door*, 142–45; Grover, *Why I Help People Take Drugs*, 23–30.

have significant weaknesses. Critics of Maté have pointed out that it can easily slide into a version of the disease model, essentially determinist and failing to emphasize the agency and resilience of the person.[3] Furthermore, significant evidence runs contrary to the claim that persons with adverse childhood experiences will necessarily develop addiction.[4] Many people who experience very significant pain and loss do not develop addictions.

Christians have additional reasons to think carefully about Maté's assertion. A foundational truth of Christian theology is that evil is nothing more than the deprivation of the good. If it is true, and I think it is, that addiction is usually a response to suffering, it is also true that addiction is a way of seeking the good things that were lost or marred in the experience of suffering. In other words, to find the *first* cause of addiction in suffering is not a deep enough insight. We need to ask the question that is deeper still: "What good, God-given desires are persons trying to satisfy, however fruitlessly, through addiction?" To answer this question, one must engage sensitively and seek to understand the pain, suffering, and dislocation within a person's story. But a full answer does not start there. The first rootedness of addiction lies in our nature as God's creatures who were made for the good. As psychologist Carl Jung, who was not a Christian, wrote: "[The addicted person's] craving for alcohol was the equivalent, on a low level, of the spiritual thirst of our being for wholeness, expressed in medieval language: the union with God."[5] In other words, alcohol addiction is not an arbitrary response to pain. It is a particular way that brokenness can cause us to look for the right things in the wrong places. Addiction is therefore a real outworking, however disordered, of our nature as God's creatures who rightly long for transcendence, ecstatic joy, and perfect peace.

To phrase this contention differently: we have become accustomed to hearing about the overwhelming potency of addictive objects. Novel synthetic drugs, gambling apps, and social media

---

3. See, for example, Peele, "Seductive, But Dangerous, Allure."
4. See Peele, "Seductive, But Dangerous, Allure."
5. Jung, *C.G. Jung Letters*, 624.

10. NATURE

algorithms are just a few examples. In some respects, such potency arguments are true. These things have terrifying power to entrap us in cycles of compulsive and ultimately destructive behavior. But Christians should also see the deeper truth that the problem with drugs, apps, and algorithms is *not* fundamentally that they are too potent or powerful for the human person. The problem is that they are not potent or powerful *enough*. These things cannot truly satiate the particular desires embedded in our nature as human persons.

The inadequacy of addictions to satisfy is a common theme in addictions memoirs. In Judith Grisel's aptly titled book, *Never Enough*, she recounts the "prophecy" of a friend: "Toward the end of that binge, the stash mercifully depleted, both of us exhausted and on edge, my friend inexplicably announced that there would never be enough cocaine for us."[6] Or similarly, in the words of someone with a pornography addiction: "I will never get enough of what doesn't satisfy me and [pornography] never, ever satisfies me."[7] The central problem is that these and other addictions do not satisfy human persons. *They cannot give us what we need.* There is more than enough cocaine and hard-core pornography in the world to destroy, but not enough to satisfy. This insight often tempts persons with addictions to despair, facing an internal abyss of pain and need that cocaine, pornography, or other addictive objects can never fill. But the insight that our addictions are not potent enough to satisfy need not lead to despair. Rightly understood, this insight can instead point us to high and beautiful truths about what it means to be a human person.

Christianity teaches that all of us were created for joy, with a particular nature that is only ultimately satisfied through union with God. The truth that addiction, even to the most potent of created things, cannot satiate reveals a common human need. For the Christian, this needfulness is not lamentable. Our need for satisfaction from outside of ourselves is beautiful and good, accordant to our nature as creatures made for relationship with God. In other words, *the internal abyss that Grisel tried to fill*

---

6. Grisel, *Never Enough*, 1.
7. Wilson, *Your Brain on Porn*, 81.

with cocaine was not an abyss at all. The deep needs that we try fruitlessly to satisfy through our addictions are not bottomless chasms of pain and emptiness. These needs are better conceptualized as a lock, for which there exists a corresponding key: the rest and joy found in the God who hates injustice and longs to heal us. The beautiful hope of the church is that God desires to fill us with the Holy Spirit, to join our lives to the divine life, and so to mend our sorrows.

So What?

How do we apply this insight to the life of Christian communities? It suggests that we ought to cultivate the patient and sensitive spaces that help persons uncover the ways that their addictions, however disordered, stem from good desires. We should be like novelist Bruce Marshall's fictional priest, Father Smith, who remarks: "the young man who rings the bell at the brothel is unconsciously looking for God."[8] To say this does not absolve the person of responsibility for the harms that their behavior causes to others. The person with pornography addiction, for example, must face the way their addiction, far from delighting in the true beauty of the human body, participates in injustice by degrading the beauty of the human person to that of a consumer object. Facing these hard truths, in something like the "moral inventory" of twelve-step programs, is a necessary part of the journey of healing. Many people remain in cycles of addiction because they cannot face these difficult realities.

How can Christian communities help these persons find the resources to take such steps? Again, by seeing beneath the destructive consequences of addiction to the true needs of the person. For example, it is true that a married father who is addicted to pornography is jeopardizing his marriage and family life in addition to disrespecting the persons depicted in the pornographic content. If

---

8. B. Marshall, *World*, 108. This quote is often misattributed to G. K. Chesterton.

10. NATURE

we accept that addiction is a phenomenon of incontinence,[9] then the person involved already knows this at some level. Reminding this person of the potentially devastating consequences of his addiction may be helpful in some cases but is insufficient in terms of promoting true healing and freedom. Rather, Christians should ask, even in cases of very disordered addictive behavior: "What good things are you seeking, underneath the obviously destructive things that you are doing? What are you *really* wanting when you want to gamble, drink, or look at pornography?" Christian communities should be committed to caring for our friends with addiction by devoting the time and gentle care necessary to help them uncover the healing answers to these questions.

Finally, considering addiction through the lens of created human nature empowers the church to be a place of hope. Our addictions cannot satiate us because we were made to be satiated by nothing other than the infinite beauty of God. This points to a key theme of the next chapter: persons with addiction do not have an additional moral problem when compared to other persons. All of us are in need of repentance and healing. This view compels us to believe and promote high and hopeful possibilities for the lives of our neighbors who carry the burden of severe addiction. The opposite of addiction is *not* a kind of white-knuckled stoic self-denial. It is not a forgoing of the good things that were sought through addiction. Rather, the opposite of addiction is a life that is completely given over to the good, true, and beautiful. Our hope for those with addiction is not merely for "abstinence," "sobriety," or "remission." Our joyful hope for their destiny is for their created nature to be satisfied and fulfilled via the infinite joy and perfect freedom of union with God.

---

9. See ch. 5.

11. Repentance

> The church should be a place where we set aside culpability judgments in favor of loving our neighbors, because we confess, "All have sinned and fall short of the glory of God."[1]

"I Confess"

I TOOK MY DAUGHTER to midnight Mass at the Catholic cathedral on Christmas Eve last year. We got there almost an hour early and barely found a seat. By 11:30, every pew was crammed full and dozens of people were standing at the back. Most were dressed formally, waiting reverently for the start of the service. I noticed two ushers watching the newcomers closely. When a visibly pregnant woman arrived one of them promptly unseated a young man and offered the space to her. I watched them do the same for an elderly couple and a family with very young children. I admired them for their cheerful and resolute willingness to unseat the suit-clad early-birds in favor of those who needed the pew space more.

Just as the pre-service hush fell over the congregation, the doors behind me swung open and a woman walked in. I smelled her before I saw her. Liquor, tobacco, and sweat. She dropped something on the floor. It clanked and rolled. She apologized loudly, stumbling and slurring. But the ushers did not pause. One of them swiftly booted a young couple to make space for her. The other

---

1. Rom 3:23.

put a hand on her back, greeted her warmly, and guided her gently to the newly vacant seat. Only then were we ready to welcome Christ. We stood and prayed: "I confess to almighty God, and to you, my brothers and sisters, that I have greatly sinned through my thoughts and in my words, in what I have done, and in what I have failed to do." Not being a Catholic, I stumbled through the words. I turned and looked at the recent arrival. She was standing, praying with the congregation, her face shining with joy. I recognized her from her visits to St. Paul's emergency department.

It struck me that participation in a shared confession of sin was not a kind of self-flagellation which further burdened this person whose life was wracked by addiction. Rather, when paired with refuge and hospitality, it produced a sense that she belonged there, seated among other sinners in need of grace. She was saying all that needed to be said to be right with God. She was like the rest of us. She was ready for Christmas. And we, praise God, were like her.

The Good News of Sin

I expect that many readers are wary of considering how the theological concept of sin relates to the behavioral category of addiction. This reluctance is usually well motivated, driven by a desire to resist simple judgmentalism and avoid culpability adjudications. These motives are good. Christians should seek frameworks that set us free to be cheerfully agnostic about culpability questions and therefore care for those with addictions simply because they are persons. Simply because they bear God's image. Perhaps counterintuitively, however, considering addiction alongside the concept of sin can actually help us, provided that we have a sufficiently nuanced understanding of sin. Confessing the predicament of addiction as one face of the universal human predicament can help the church be a place of meaningful recovery. It is, of course, beyond the scope of this book to consider a comprehensive theology of sin. But for this discussion, it will be sufficient to see—like we saw with the choice and disease

SECTION 3: ADDICTION AND THE LIFE OF THE CHURCH

concepts of addiction in section 1—how mediating between voluntarist and determinist definitions will produce a more theologically precise and helpful understanding of sin.

The first reason that the category of sin might seem irrelevant to addiction is rooted in the already-discussed misunderstanding of what addiction is. The determinist, medical, disease model suggests that addiction is not a moral issue at all. If addiction is no different from type-one diabetes, then to ask questions of sin is to make a category mistake. As considered in section 1, these models purport to be compassionate but ultimately lack explanatory power and respect for persons. A personal model of addiction engages the more complex truths that addiction is about meaning, ordering one's life, and seeking goods. In other words, it is inescapably a moral issue.

The second reason why the concept of sin might seem irrelevant to addiction is rooted in a misunderstanding of what sin is. An aversion to the language of sin often arises from the idea that labeling a behavior as sinful is to make culpability judgments about the person involved. But, if our understanding of sin is sufficiently nuanced, this is not the case.

Just as with addiction, there are determinist and voluntarist understandings of sin that purport to explain the relation of the individual will to a given behavior. At the determinist extreme is the belief that all sin is involuntary, produced by evil forces that act through human beings. One form of this idea, called Manichaeism, was condemned by the early church as a heresy. At the voluntarist extreme is the belief that sin is only a matter of willful wrongdoing and human perfection can be achieved through the exercise of will alone. In the early church, this was condemned as the Pelagian heresy. Just as with addiction, each of these poles is inadequate in terms of explanatory power and respect for persons.

A theologically orthodox understanding of sin, like a rich understanding of addiction, mediates between these flawed extremes. Sin is not only a matter of willful wrongdoing. It describes the wounded nature and disordered loves that causally precede individual human actions. It names the systems of injustice that

11. REPENTANCE

subvert and distort our attempts to pursue the good. And, it relates to the entrapping pressures that inhibit our ability to grasp the good things God intends for us. Sin is a moral relational term, referencing that which mars our right relationships with God, other human persons, and the natural world.

If we understand sin in this way, we can begin to see why there is nothing about addiction that falls outside of what Christians have always confessed about the universal human need for grace and healing. As Dunnington writes: "When we speak of addiction in the theological category of sin, we draw attention to the way in which addiction constitutes not a moral deficiency but rather a falling away from our perfect good of eternal friendship with God."[2] Describing addictive behaviors in terms of sin can therefore clarify and ground our moral rebellion against the harms of addiction. Rather than suggesting negative judgments about the person with addiction, this insight focuses Christians on the truth that they were made for more.

Willingness to consider addiction through the lens of sin gives us language to see how persons with addiction do not have an *additional* moral problem when compared to other persons. They do not have an extra moral problem in addition to the universal predicament that Christians call sin. This understanding is critical for churches. Persons with addiction often feel unwelcome in Christian communities. They do not find that their need to be freed from addiction is subsumed within a shared confession of frailty and need. It is not surprising, then, that twelve-step communities, which are grounded on common confession, are more recognizable as places of refuge and hospitality. Alcoholics Anonymous, for example, famously encourages persons to narrate their introductions in the terms of a common confession: "My name is Casey, and I am an alcoholic." This practice grounds the people around the circle—those whose last drink was yesterday and those whose last drink was twenty years ago—in what they share. There may be good reasons for Christians to question the language of this practice, precisely because to confess

---

2. Dunnington, *Addiction and Virtue*, 140.

oneself as a sinner emphasizes commonality with *all* persons while including within itself all that needs to be confessed, morally speaking, about the person's addiction. In other words, it is a "much more radical attribution" than the confession of being an "alcoholic."³ With that being said, Christian communities have much to learn from this AA practice in terms of how grounding our communities in shared confession can actually make us places of refuge, hospitality, and friendship. To reference the story that I started this chapter with: the unity of those participating in that Christmas Mass was not based on shared status, wealth, cultural background, virtue, health, or social standing. Meaningful unity arose from shared confession of sin.

We have already seen that choice and disease models of addiction share a culpability-care premise that Christians should reject in favor of an ethic of care, friendship, and love. Addiction is one of many moral phenomena that reveals how all human communities and individuals have fallen away from the freedom that God made us for. We can see this clearly while also being agnostic about the culpability of persons in individual cases. The language of sin, when understood in neither simply voluntarist nor determinist terms, provides us with a way to articulate this truth. Although the language of sin has become unfashionable in our cultural context and even within many churches, confession of sin is a necessary step for all of us in growing toward the good. Moreover, Christian communities that are founded on confessions of shared sin and frailty are empowered to be places of meaningful refuge, hospitality, and friendship for those with addiction.

Finally, confession of shared sin empowers the church to be a place of hope. Everyone agrees that addiction is one face of the *something* that is wrong with the world as we encounter it. Regardless of where people locate the causes of addiction's devastating consequences, everyone agrees that our current addictions crisis represents a falling away from how things ought to be. We feel in our bones that *things should be different*. Rightly understood, this moral rebellion against the suffering of those with addiction

---

3. Dunnington, *Addiction and Virtue*, 185.

is a signpost that should point us to God. As theologian Jürgen Moltmann writes: "grief over life that is destroyed is nothing other than an ardent longing for life's liberation to happiness and joy. Otherwise we would accept innocent suffering and destroyed life as our fate and destiny."[4] If we, human agents and societies, are the powerless victims of addiction, then there is no meaningful hope for healing. If the problem is not with us but with reality itself, then our work to produce communities of peace and justice is destined to be futile. But, if the problem is a moral problem, with us as individuals and societies, then there is good hope that we might one day be reconciled to an ultimate reality that is perfectly good and infinitely free. That reality is called God.

---

4. Moltmann, "Christianity," 14.

12. Order

> The church should be a place where misordered lives can be reordered through love of God and, therefore, where addictions can be displaced through a cooperative effort between the individual will, communities of grace, and the work of the Holy Spirit.

Addiction and Disorder, Again

IN THE FIRST COMMANDMENT, God tells the people of Israel, "Have no other gods before me."[1] Set all your other allegiances beneath right relation to God. Place your loves in the right order. All the following commandments could be articulated in terms of this first one. To break any of them is to love or serve something as a god that is not the true God.

Jesus emphasizes this same theme when asked to sum up the law in terms of a greatest commandment: "You shall love the Lord your God with all your heart and with all your soul and with all your mind."[2] The simplest way to describe the good life, for a Christian, is to say it is what grows from loving God first with our whole selves. When we love created things for God's sake, we love them in the ways that allow them to produce goods. When we love them above God, "out of order," our relationship

---

1. Exod 20:3.
2. Matt 22:37.

with them becomes distorted and erodes their ability to produce good things in our lives.

Addiction is one face of the universal human problem: loving created things in disordered and disordering ways. Addiction is powerful because it provides persons with ways of seeking real goods, for example, courage, joy, hope, comfort, belonging, and peace. Addiction is harmful because the addictive behavior cannot ultimately produce these goods. Moreover, it is harmful because it erodes the person's ability to seek them in more fruitful places. Effective approaches to recovery therefore do not understand recovery simply in terms of stopping the harmful behavior, as if an ordering principle could be replaced with nothing. Rather, the journey of finding freedom from addiction is one form of the sanctifying journey that is shared by all Christians. If addiction is one face of the universal human problem, then it follows that recovery is one face of the common solution: displacing disordered patterns with the ordering love of God.

Christian communities can be attentive to the unique features of different addictions while also seeing how recovery from addiction has much in common with other forms of healing and sanctification. The church should therefore be empowered to be a place of healing for addiction because we are all walking a similar path of discipline, accountability, reconciliation, and joyful growth toward the good, true, and beautiful. We should all be journeying from incontinence, through continence, to Godly virtue.

This chapter considers how the process of recovery from addiction, like other forms of sanctification, is a re-ordering process that involves development of individual agency, immersion in communities of grace, and the transformative work of the Holy Spirit. Despite the entrapping power of severe addiction, the freeing power of such a cooperative process is greater still.

Development of Personal Agency

A personal model of addiction suggests that the development of personal agency is a necessary component of recovery. Sustained recovery is unlikely unless the affected person's will can be empowered to overcome compulsions and produce continent, then virtuous, behavior. Recalling the parable of the father's two lost sons, a necessary part of the younger son's redemption journey is leaving the pigs and placing one foot in front of the other as he traveled along the path toward home. We can speak precisely and respectfully about persons with addiction by saying that they remain moral agents with capacity for this kind of resilience and courage. We all, however, need help on the road. Those with addiction need help developing the individual agency that will enable a life that is ordered according to love of God. How can the church foster this kind of agency?

We have already considered one essential answer to this question: friendship. More specifically, friendship with mature sisters and brothers who have similar life experiences, weaknesses, or wounds. These relationships provide concrete examples from which those who are nearer the beginning of a healing journey can learn. Friendship should produce forms of hospitality that address a given person's particular needs: a space reserved at *this* supper table, *this* phone always left on at night in case help is needed, or *this* home wherein everyone has cheerfully agreed not to drink alcohol so as to help a beloved guest avoid temptation.

Christian communities should also promote individual agency by providing opportunities for those with addiction to serve, lead, build, and create. In my experience, Christian communities do not want to further burden those with addiction or other significant needs, so we may be hesitant to invite them to mutual participation. We say, "You can come here and simply *be*." But, without minimizing the importance of safe refuge, such an approach has limited power to displace addiction. Yes, we should welcome people as they are. But we should then invite them to immersive involvement as mutual participants in the life of an ordering community. As a friend with severe addiction once told me: "If addicts looking for recovery are going to leave the church, it won't be because the church asks too much of them. It will be because it asks too little." In other words, churches can be places

12. ORDER

of recovery by offering daily ways by which persons can be immersed in new forms of responsibility, interpersonal engagement, and creativity. When we do so, we will find our communities blessed and challenged by the example of our brothers and sisters who are on journeys of recovery from addiction.

I have a pastor friend who planted a church several years ago. The church community he had come from was mostly comprised of professionals and young families. He assumed that the congregants of the new church plant would come from similar demographics. But, through God's abundant grace, my friend has found himself pastoring a church that reflects the demographics of a neighborhood where addiction is a common and visible issue. He has found that persons in recovery from addiction, when given the opportunity, are among the most committed to leading and serving, to sustaining the life of a small church in a city where Christianity is uncommon and unpopular. My friend has struggled, at times, to find sufficient opportunities to quench their keenness to be involved in as many ways as possible. Sometimes the entire worship band is comprised of men who live in a recovery facility. One says that he came to faith in Christ that way, "playing the keyboard at the front." My friend has found that these sisters and brothers often want intensity—consuming immersion in worship and daily rhythms of community life—that some congregants prefer to avoid. He has found the passionate engagement of persons in recovery to challenge the all-too-common consumeristic ways in which many of us participate in church communities. When this is true, those in recovery from addiction can be powerful moral examples who challenge others by modeling what it is to seek total surrender to the consuming mercy of God. When we are willing to ask much of those seeking recovery from addiction, we will often find them to be extraordinary instruments of God's blessing and examples in the journey of discipleship. Further, doing so empowers the agency of those in recovery by revealing their personal capacity to be leaders and by re-ordering their time and relationships around the potency of vibrant human community.

SECTION 3: ADDICTION AND THE LIFE OF THE CHURCH

Personal agency can also be promoted by helping individuals explore and develop their particular gifts and vocations. One of the most powerful ways to displace addiction is to participate in other things that produce the goods that were previously sought through addiction. To some degree, there will be common themes—creativity, human connection, responsibility—in the activities that allow people to access these goods. At the same time, these practices will be based on an individual's gifts and experiences. For example, poet Christian Wiman writes, "I have been addicted to opiates in my life and I must say that there is a kinship between that flood of sane and amiable elation that opiates engender and the release of *meaning* when the right sounds are linked together."[3] In other words, the practice of writing poetry offers Wiman a healthier way of finding that same good thing he previously sought through addiction to opioids.

I suspect many of us struggle to relate to the specific "meaning-making" kinship between consuming opioids and writing poetry. That is, I think, only because most of us are not poets. But I hope all of us can relate to the experience of finding meaning and joy when we are totally immersed in a task that we feel we were made to do. For me, teaching sometimes feels like that. Playing the drums. A smooth procedural sedation for the reduction of a dislocated shoulder. Hunting for crabs with my children. Writing, occasionally. These practices are rooted in my own unique story and giftings. Provided they are ordered under the love of God, they help me displace wrongly ordered loves and seek the good for myself and others. I needed the help of many mentors and friends to discover and develop the practices that direct my own giftings and passions toward loving God and my neighbors. All of us do. Christian communities can promote recovery by helping those with addiction discern and develop particular vocations that grow from their unique stories and gifts. As Wiman's quote suggests, these practices can displace addiction by offering ways of finding meaning in more fruitful places.

---

3. Wiman, *Zero at the Bone*, 92. Emphasis is mine.

Finally, we can promote agency, and therefore recovery, by being a community that invites persons to live the Christian story through the practices of baptism, liturgy, Bible study, Sabbath-keeping, fasting, funerals, and more. Agency, for all of us, brings freedom only when it means ever-increasing ability to live our lives in alignment with God's particular story of rescue. How does the power of communities of grace promote recovery from addiction?

Communities of Grace

The church can promote reordering of life, and therefore displacement of addiction, through practices, including baptism and communion, that bring each individual to the grace of God. In my experience, we often miss the centrality of these practices when we talk about addiction. Praxis-focused Christians often see grace primarily in terms of the kindness and humility that community members should have when with engaging one another. These virtues are important, of course. But the Christian community is not founded on certain kinds of human interactions, however beautiful they may be. To call the church a community of grace is not primarily to say that it is welcoming, friendly, or even immersive. To be a community of grace is to be a place that brings persons to Jesus, where grace is found. To be a community of grace is not to accept people on their own terms, but rather to accept them on the terms of the Incarnation, where God rescues sinners. It invites not only belonging at a table, but belonging at *this particular table*, the table of communion. It compels the (usually) literally immersive ritual of baptism.

What does this have to do with the reordering of lives that have been disordered by addiction? It is worth considering one more reflection from Wiman here, this time on his sister's journey of recovery:

> The moment my father died, my sister, whose addiction to drugs had destroyed her entire adult life, stopped using. It was as if the instant she touched the one death we

all share . . . all the lesser deaths lost their charge. Not that it was easy. She shouted and shook and vomited and moved through a solitude so black that her funeral clothes seemed liked a reprieve. For days she sat out on the porch of my mother's apartment clenching her knees as if parts of herself might fly off in the wind. But slowly, week by week, the talons that for decades had gripped her loosened, and her soul slipped free. And brightened.[4]

Both baptism and communion are particular ways of practicing what is described in this powerful story: touching "the one death we all share." They therefore have tremendous power to frame all the "lesser deaths" of recovery—withdrawal, fear, doubts about the future, loneliness, facing the grief that addiction resulted from and the grief that it caused—in such a way that makes the person more able to face them. I am not suggesting that baptism and communion will feel the same as the experience that Wiman's sister had. Of course not. But Christians believe that to be baptized is *no less* of a rupture of one's life than this kind of an event. To receive communion is *no less* a real touching of the death we all share, no less an upheaval that re-orders our lives around itself. As such, and in addition to the creation of thick social networks of interdependence, churches can promote the displacement of addiction by offering baptism and communion to those who seek them. Furthermore, we should narrate these practices, and other key rhythms of religious life, in ways that draw connections between God's love for us and the needs of persons with addiction.

The Work of the Holy Spirit

Like everyone else, persons with addiction need to work to develop their own agency as part of growing toward the good. Like everyone else, persons with addiction belong in immersive communities that seek to enhance their human freedom by helping them discover their gifts and develop their vocations. Churches should know how to bring persons with addiction into the rhythms of

4. Wiman, *Zero at the Bone*, 166.

12. ORDER

religious life, believing in the real re-ordering potency of regular rhythms of worship, prayer, communion, and more. But all these efforts are not enough to make any of us good. In all of these things, we are utterly dependent on the work of the Holy Spirit, who infuses virtue in us as we seek to love God.

Christian communities have the theological tools to point persons with addiction to more than the general idea of a "higher power." We can direct our friends to a *person* of the Godhead. The Holy Spirit is a comfort and guide, through whom God's infinite freedom to rescue human beings is worked out among us. This is good news, because it situates our lives within a hopeful framework that affirms God's unyielding mercy, not our fallible efforts, as the foundation of all journeys toward the good. Saint Augustine conceptualizes this idea beautifully through the image of a person both running a race and being carried: "Look, you're here, freeing us from our unhappy wandering, setting us firmly on your track, comforting us and saying, 'Run the race! I'll carry you! I'll carry you clear to the end, and even at the end, I'll carry you.'"[5] Ultimately, none of us have the willpower or capacity to totally re-orient our lives according to the good. We are not strong. We are weak. But in our weakness God is strong.

---

5. Quoted in Smith, *On the Road*, 15.

13. Belonging

> The church should—for God's sake and by the work of the Holy Spirit—be a place of primary social belonging that offers daily support to people who need it.

I RECENTLY GAVE A talk about addiction at a church in Vancouver. A young man came up afterward to speak to me. He said he was not a Christian but he had heard about the event from his neighbor. He told me he had been addicted to cocaine for several years and his addiction was starting to destroy his work life and personal relationships. He was thinking about trying to quit but he did not know how to begin on the road to recovery. "I'm looking for a foothold." I was grateful to hear that he loved the session, finding the tone of "all you religious people" to be compassionate, personalizing, and hopeful. He told me, "I really wanted to focus, so I snuck out to the lobby at break for a bump [of cocaine]." He grinned cheekily. I wondered if there was a hint of a test there. How would the religious people respond to the knowledge that someone was snorting cocaine in their house of worship?

I told him we were happy and grateful he was there. Truly, what a gift it was that after he snuck out to use cocaine, he felt comfortable enough to come back inside! Even to tell us about it. He and I chatted a bit more and then he left. He told me that when he was ready to quit, he would come back.

This encounter was a gift. Like most good gifts, it has challenged and stretched me. I am grateful that this person perceived

13. BELONGING

the church to be a place of hospitality and potential friendship. I am also grateful that he felt we did not hold ourselves above or apart from him even though he had a severe addiction. But I am challenged by the limitations of what we will have to offer him if he returns to our doors in the future. It would not be enough to invite him to weekly religious services or offer a few meetings with a Christian minister. This young man will need new daily rhythms and practices. He will need a new place of primary social belonging, since his existing social circle is ordered around using cocaine and other intoxicants. Are our church communities organized in such a way that we are prepared to readily support the needs of persons like this?

In Acts 2, the early Christian church is characterized as a community that gathers daily. "Day by day, as they spent much time together in the temple, they broke bread at home and ate their food with glad and generous hearts."[1] This passage from Scripture presents beautiful evidence of the strength of the early Christian community. But I think it would be a mistake to assume that our first-century sisters and brothers met together because they were somehow stronger in faith or perseverance than we are. Maybe some of them needed to meet daily because their faith was weak, because they were afraid of persecution, or because they were prone to forgetting the call of God and turning instead to disordered rhythms. This would not diminish the beauty of their daily gathering. If anything, considering this should strengthen our admiration of this faith community. I believe we need to learn from this biblical example and shape our church communities as places of primary social belonging that offer practical daily support to those who need it. We have already considered key components of this kind of belonging for persons with addiction: friendship, immersion in communities of costly grace, hospitality, initiation into daily and weekly rhythms of religious life, and investment in communities of practical interdependence. In this chapter, we focus on two other groups who often suffer as a result of addiction and who also need daily support and care from the

1. Acts 2:46.

church: families affected by addiction and people whose vocation involves caring for those with addiction.

Families and Other Loved Ones

Loving someone with a severe addiction is excruciatingly difficult. Despite the existence of dedicated support groups and the publication of recent memoirs that include their perspectives,[2] the suffering of family members and close friends of persons with addiction is often invisible and isolating. Parents come home to find that their son, who they know to be gentle and kind, has broken a window and stolen from them. Every phone call could be the call that their witty and courageous daughter has overdosed. Family members often feel ashamed and guilty. David Sheff, whose son had a severe amphetamine addiction, writes: "Even as all the experts kindly tell the parents of addicts, 'You didn't cause it,' I have not let myself off the hook. I often feel as if I completely failed my son. In admitting this, I am not looking for sympathy or absolution, but instead stating a truth that will be recognized by most parents who have been through this."[3] Spouses find that their partner has gambled away the house or spent their life savings on pornography. They feel embarrassed, disbelieving, and angry. Children are devastated to discover their parent's hidden addiction. They struggle to know how to relate and how to understand their childhood in light of their parent's hidden behaviors.

The biggest mistake I have made in teaching about addiction is failing to consistently speak to the needs of these persons. In my desire to have a high view of those with addiction, to soberly consider the ways their lives call ours into question, I have sometimes placed further burdens on already heavy-laden sisters and brothers. In trying to call our communities to a high standard of self-emptying hospitality, I have sometimes wounded parents whose desire to protect younger children has led to the difficult

---

2. See, for example, D. Sheff, *Beautiful Boy*; and Wexler, *All Bets Are Off*.
3. D. Sheff, *Beautiful Boy*, 15.

13. BELONGING

decision to change their locks. In calling us to our responsibility to embody the welcome of the Father, I have sometimes failed to comfort those who would do anything to help their loved one with addiction, but who cannot because they do not know where their beloved one is. I have often failed to recognize and celebrate the wonderful and incredibly costly ways that loved ones are already working out the Father's welcome in complex and difficult circumstances. Through conversation with friends who have been affected by others' addiction, I am learning to pay closer attention to *all* the persons affected by addiction in my daily life, work as a physician, and teaching.

A mature church community will be attentive to the needs of families affected by addiction, offering refuge, belonging, and practical help. If churches want to be communities of recovery from addiction, we need to be places where families and other loved ones can be seen and embraced, where their loyalty and perseverance is recognized and celebrated, where their sorrows are beheld in compassionate tenderness, and where someone will come and fix their broken window and help them wrestle with whether or not to change the locks.

People with Caring Vocations

I am frequently asked how I sustain the health of my own soul while working in a place like St. Paul's emergency department. This question is also discussed regularly in the corridors of St. Paul's. Most emergency physicians and nurses report high levels of burnout and "compassion fatigue." In secular settings, "professional distance" is often presented as the solution to these problems. Compassionate closeness to patients is seen as potentially erosive to the long-term well-being of the caregiver. Instead of being taught how to handle the grief intrinsic to a caring vocation, medical education often suggests that "objective" distance from patients is the way to avoid burnout. I was taught that the way to a sustainable vocation was to "down-regulate the appropriate aspects of empathy so as to avoid burnout and compassion fatigue, while ensuring that [you are] still capable [of] eliciting an empathic response strong enough to be motivated to assist patients as needed."[4] In this framework, compassion is a kind of necessary evil. We must have enough to build trust with suffering patients, but we should regard it as dangerous to ourselves. As philosopher Friedrich Nietzsche, who famously despised Christian compassion, wrote: "We are deprived of strength when we feel pity.... Pity makes suffering contagious."[5]

It is not difficult to see how such a formulation actually promotes the emotional deadening that people often describe as burnout. There is a sad irony here. The strong emphasis on professional distance from those who suffer actually harms caregivers by distancing them from the very things that make caring vocations meaningful: opportunities to demonstrate compassion and care for persons in need. The most fruitful, if incredibly difficult, response to feelings of burnout is to seek closeness to, not distance from, other persons.

Further, Christians should feel a specific moral imperative here: it is simply *wrong* to aspire to stand distant from those who suffer, even when working in professional settings. Because Christ emptied himself on behalf of every human person, we should recognize each member of the human family as deserving of close compassionate care. It would therefore be morally outrageous for me to be unmoved when I witness the tragic death of a human person, who was created and loved by God and bore the divine image. Who would want to think that their physician was unmoved by their suffering?

But if Nietzsche was wrong to reject compassion, he was right that the practice of compassion, literally "co-suffering," is

---

4. Gleichgerrcht and Decety, "Relationship Between Different Facets of Empathy," 8.

5. Nietzsche, "Antichrist," 572–73. In contemporary contexts, it is common to distinguish between compassion and pity, the latter notion seen as less desirable because it is potentially condescending. But Nietzsche, here, is not referencing this kind of distinction; the "pity" notion he is criticizing is what we would call Christian compassion. In addition, it is worth noting that, etymologically at least, pity and compassion are synonyms.

13. BELONGING

costly. This is certainly true of my experience as an emergency physician. I relate to what theologian Stanley Hauerwas wrote in his essay on medicine and the church: "The physician cannot help but be touched . . . by the world of the sick. Through their willingness to be present to us in our most vulnerable moments they are forever scarred with our pain."[6] Although I do not feel burned out, I am wounded by the suffering of my patients with addiction. I believe that to aspire to anything other than such woundedness would be wrong. I believe that, in the light of the work of Christ, these kinds of scars and wounds are gifts. I pray for the humility necessary to give my wounds to Jesus, that they may become—like the wounds on his palms, feet, and side—scars that testify to the power of God to save.

But how do we bear the wounds that come from our vocations? How can we follow theologian Nicholas Wolterstoff's exhortation: "The stoics of antiquity said: Be calm. Disengage yourself. Neither laugh nor weep. Jesus says: Be open to the wounds of the world. Mourn humanity's mourning, weep over humanity's weeping, be wounded by humanity's wounds, be in agony over humanity's agony. But do so in the good cheer that a day of peace is coming"?[7]

For me, the core answer to this question is that I belong to a church community. Not just that "I go to church." I *belong* among a group of frail and dependent persons who narrate our lives in terms of our common need for one another and for God. This community is a refuge for me, where my grief over the suffering of my patients is not pathologized or interpreted as a failure of professional performance. Rather, to use the provocative words of philosopher Ivan Illich, the life of my church community "makes pain tolerable by interpreting its necessity."[8] The church can serve persons with caring vocations by speaking the truth about the grief our vocations should produce and by expecting us to need comfort, care, and compassion. Furthermore, the lives of my

---

6. Hauerwas, "Salvation and Health," 49.
7. Wolterstorff, *Lament for a Son*, 86.
8. Illich, *Limits to Medicine*, 134.

sisters and brothers with different vocations can contextualize the difficulties of my work within a thick social and moral space that renders them as intelligible and redeemable.

A few months ago, I watched my friend Jenn receive communion on a Sunday morning. Jenn was pregnant and scheduled for delivery at the hospital the next morning. Jenn's child had been diagnosed in utero with a complex congenital vascular abnormality. Jenn and her husband, Josiah, had been told that their beloved child's prognosis was uncertain. Nevertheless, they loved and celebrated their child's presence as a gift from God. They did not know, taking communion on that Sunday, how long their child would survive after labor and delivery. They had not set up a crib or taken out any baby clothes, knowing that they may not be bringing a child home that week. In the midst of this uncertainty and fear, they were at church. Jenn was receiving the body of Christ into her own body, which in turn held the fragile body of her son. As I watched her partake in the Lord's supper that Sunday morning, I was awed and humbled by her courage, radical hospitality, and faith in the sufficiency of God's goodness. When I am struggling to bear what I cannot bear, to continue in a costly and self-emptying vocation, I often think about Jenn. Although our experiences are, of course, far from the same, her example is a gift to my work at St. Paul's. I aspire to display a fraction of the hospitality, courage, and grace in my physician vocation that Jenn and Josiah have displayed in their vocation as parents.

I could share many more examples of the ways that my sisters and brothers sustain and contextualize the life of my vocation through their example and care for me. I am deeply grateful for this. But there is one critical caveat: there is nothing unique about my local church that is not available to any other Christian community. We are fools and frail sinners, subject to the same temptations and human social dynamics as anyone. Despite this, God's Holy Spirit has made my own church a space that has offered rich gifts to me and my family.

In summary, I am sustained in my vocation by belonging to a community of faith that offers me regular opportunities to serve, share, care, listen, play music, eat, teach, and be taught. The church should be attentive to the ways that vocations involving care of addicted persons can, and should, produce grief and suffering. Perhaps counterintuitively, churches can care for persons not by trying to free them from grief but rather by helping them understand that their grief can be a gift that is part of God's redeeming of the world. We can help them bear grief through compassion, co-suffering with them as they co-suffer with their addicted patients, clients, or friends. And we can tell them the truth that a day of peace is coming.

14. Recovery

> The church should affirm policy options, medical therapies, counseling and support programs, and other interventions that aim at displacing addiction, without abandoning its responsibility to be a place of belonging and truth.

MOST OF THE CONVERSATIONS I have about addiction begin with someone bringing up policy proposals or specific "frontline" measures that aim to address the issue in one way or another. What do I think about harm reduction? The Portugal model? Safe(r) supply? Involuntary treatment? What about Suboxone? Methadone? Prescription heroin? Farm-based rehabilitation? Needle-exchange programs? Criminalization or de-criminalization? Twelve-step programs? Training high-school students to administer naloxone? Supervised consumption sites?

These are pressing, nuanced, and often difficult questions. They can feel like proverbial "elephants in the room" in all our conversations about addiction. Although we may not know how to address these relevant questions directly, we know they cannot be avoided. I would guess many readers, especially those who care for persons with drug addictions, have felt the presence of these elephants throughout this book. How does a personal model help Christians think about practical questions relating to addictions care? Where is the "so what?" in all of this for our front-line work with our vulnerable neighbors?

14. RECOVERY

My first response is that we have already encountered most of the "so what?" in prior chapters. We should primarily respond to the addiction crisis in the same way as the church should respond to all crises of all times: by being the church, "a community that signifies, that points to a possible healed human world."[1] What are we *doing* about the addiction crisis? We are confessing our sins, welcoming strangers into our homes, making friends, receiving communion, practicing uncalculated giving and graceful receiving, enjoying the beautiful, worshiping together, and co-suffering with our suffering neighbors. These practices are not abstractly spiritual. They are pragmatic ways of promoting reorder and recovery.

At the same time, the life of the church should produce the intellectual clarity and conviction necessary to speak about public and secular interventions that seek the good for those with addiction. The present chapter is devoted to a framework for how a personal model of addiction and the intellectual freedom of the Christian can empower us to address the difficult questions of addictions interventions.

To examine how the church can do this, we will first consider two insufficient approaches. First, believing that the church cannot speak to or about these things. Second, at the opposite extreme, viewing the church as a kind of totalizing alternative that renders other spaces unhelpful or even opposed to the purposes of God's kingdom. It will then be possible to consider a richer third way, which emphasizes the freedom of the church to humbly serve and support that which promotes the good without losing sight of its own responsibility to be a place of primary belonging and prophetic truth. I will then offer a framework through which Christians can think about public interventions that purport to promote the good for our neighbors with addiction.

---

1. Williams, *Faith in the Public Square*, 61.

SECTION 3: ADDICTION AND THE LIFE OF THE CHURCH

Two Pitfalls and a Middle Way

This section began by considering a mother and father seeking advice from a minister with regard to the severe addiction of their son. The parents in this case were unsure of the Christian view of opioid replacement therapies and twelve-step programs. It is a victory of Christian hospitality when people facing this type of difficult scenario are willing to come to Christian leaders and friends for advice and help. We have the responsibility to respond to their need with uncalculated giving, part of which is the giving of meaningfully helpful counsel.

The first inadequate approach to these parents might be called the "just talk to your doctor approach." Recall the first answers given by the seminarians when I presented this scenario to them. This approach suggests that this family's questions regarding addictions interventions are questions without theological import. The "just talk to your doctor approach" assumes a dualistic view of persons that sees addiction as a narrowly medical problem and the church as a place for spiritual care only. The implication, if the medical and the spiritual are taken to be entirely separate domains, is that the life of the church cannot shed light on treatment or recovery interventions. A Christian who accepted this view might therefore seek to offer spiritual support to the suffering persons but defer questions of recovery to other spaces.

The "just talk to your doctor approach" is not a sufficient response to addressing the needs of our addicted neighbors and their family. Addiction is not a narrow medical condition. It is a *whole person* phenomenon. Any attempt to neatly divide the experience of addicted persons into medical and spiritual categories is therefore unhelpful and even misleading. Moreover, the practices of mature church communities *really* do address the deepest and most significant factors that promote recovery from addiction. Christian leaders should therefore be empowered and responsible, using something like the framework proposed later in this chapter, to help families parse the pros and cons of approaches such as harm reduction, opioid replacement therapies, and twelve-step programs. To recede from this challenging task into the "just talk to your doctor approach" is easier but fails to do enough to help those who come to us with need. More fundamentally, it fails to recognize the beautiful ways that the Christian story speaks to the nature of addiction and the nature of freedom.

An equally inadequate approach to counseling this family might be called the "don't talk to your doctor approach." In this scenario, the minister who is advising these parents suggests, directly or indirectly, that interventions outside the life of the church community are alternatives to belonging within the church. The "don't talk to your doctor approach" implies that secular interventions should be viewed with suspicion or even hostility. In this view, the sufficiency of Gospel truth is taken to mean that any interventions outside of confessionally Christian contexts are unnecessary, or even opposed to justice, peace, and freedom. I suspect this kind of perspective is less common than the first pitfall we have considered, especially in cases of severe addiction to drugs. Nonetheless, it is present in some Christian conversations around addiction.[2]

The most obvious weakness of the "don't talk to your doctor approach" is that it does not align with the considerable evidence that some interventions outside of confessionally Christian spaces can successfully promote real goods for persons with addiction. For example, twelve-step programs often produce rich friendships, reconciliation, and long-term recovery.[3] Further, some medical and social interventions that are commonly called harm reduction measures reduce the overdose and infectious disease risks associated with drug use.[4] If we care about persons with addiction, we should not be dismissive of these real goods and the potential of secular and public spaces to produce them. Rather, we should see such spaces as potential partners in the

---

2. See, for example: Welch, "Letter to an Alcoholic."

3. See Kelly et al., "Alcoholics Anonymous"; and Kaskutas, "Alcoholics Anonymous Effectiveness."

4. See B. D. L. Marshall et al., "Reduction in Overdose Mortality"; and Abdul-Quader et al., "Effectiveness of Structural-Level Needle/Syringe Programs."

work of promoting recovery and freedom. Christian communities should enrich these spaces by investing time and service into them, believing these contexts can be vehicles of grace for vulnerable persons. Doing so requires a willingness to wrestle with the ethical and practical challenges of potential interventions that seek to promote the good for those with addiction.

The two pitfalls we have just considered share a common feature. Each situates the public questions of addressing addiction as outside the scope of what the church should speak to. The first pitfall doubts the sufficiency of the Christian story to address contemporary questions about addictions interventions. The second pitfall misunderstands what the sufficiency of the Christian story suggests. Each of these viewpoints fails to see how the true sufficiency of the Christian story compels us to freely engage the difficult questions of addictions care with humility, conviction, and clarity. The freedom of Christian communities should not be merely a freedom *from* public, pluralistic, or secular spaces. Rather, Christian freedom is freedom *for* these spaces. It is freedom to celebrate and learn from them when they do good work, to perceive God's grace at work through them when they promote justice and peace, and to serve them humbly. Critically, the Christian is free to do these things without placing ultimate hope in the power of policy, medicine, or support groups to save persons.

To summarize, neither the "just talk to your doctor approach" nor the "don't talk to your doctor approach" does enough to help our friends with addiction who need the care of the church. Instead, Christians should pick up the difficult task of considering *how* and *why* proposed interventions, including those suggested in public or secular settings, do or do not promote the good. We should humbly learn from spaces outside the church when they produce healing and freedom from addiction. For example, I believe that most churches need to be *more* like twelve-step communities in the ways that they are intentionally structured to promote friendship, provide opportunities for daily gathering, and narrate life in terms of shared frailty and need. At the same time, the church should maintain the clarity to identify instances when well-motivated interventions do not successfully promote freedom, recovery, and healing.

In the remainder of this chapter, I propose two guiding questions that will enable us to connect our core theological convictions to frontline conversations about the addiction crisis. When assessing interventions that purport to seek the good for persons with addiction, Christians should ask: (1) *Does the intervention recognize that addiction is opposed to the good?* and (2) *Does the intervention have a high enough hope for persons?*

We will consider harm reduction measures as an example of how to apply these questions to contemporary conversations. To use this example, it is necessary to briefly outline what this phrase means. "Harm reduction" most specifically refers to interventions that aim at reducing the risks associated with drug use, even if the means of doing so involve passively or actively facilitating the use of drugs. Common examples of harm reduction interventions include supervised consumption sites (sometimes called "safe injection sites" or "overdose prevention sites") or needle exchange programs. There are challenges to using the general language of harm reduction. It is semantically positioning language, implicitly suggesting that those who oppose these kinds of interventions are somehow pro-harm. This phrase is closed to good-faith arguments that simply weigh harm and benefit in different ways. In addition, the application of the term "harm reduction" has broadened in many contexts to include a wide range of interventions. For example, under the umbrella of a harm reduction approach some people would include both uncomplicatedly good actions (such as distributing naloxone for reversal of life-threatening opioid overdoses) and very controversial interventions (such as administering "safer supply" opioids to persons who are known to be diverting them).[5] The most helpful initial step is to resist a polarized all-or-nothing approach to harm reduction and instead to parse the pros and cons of individual interventions as graciously and precisely as possible. In the following paragraphs harm reduction is explored in light of our two guiding questions.

5. See, for example: Bird et al., "Clinicians' Perspectives."

SECTION 3: ADDICTION AND THE LIFE OF THE CHURCH

Does the Intervention Recognize That Addiction Is Opposed to the Good?

According to a personal model, addiction is a phenomenon that is necessarily opposed to the good for human persons. This is not because Christians are grumpy anti-pleasure moralizers but because we are in favor of patterns that actually satisfy the needs that accord to our created nature. It would therefore be more correct (although not entirely precise) to say we oppose addiction because we are pro-pleasure than to say we oppose addiction because we are anti-pleasure. Addiction is powerful because it is a way of looking for the good things God made us for. Addiction is destructive because it cannot deliver those good things and, moreover, because it eclipses our ability to participate in the good things in life. The problem with addiction is not just the risks associated with many addictive behaviors. Addiction entraps persons in cycles of disorder that necessarily tend toward tragedy. If loving someone fundamentally means wanting the good for them, then loving an addicted person means aspiring to their freedom from addiction, because addiction inhibits their participation in the good, true, and beautiful.

If this is true, then we should critique arguments and interventions that obscure or deny the necessarily harmful nature of addiction. One example of this kind of argument can be found in Meera Grover's recent book: *Why I Help People Take Drugs*. Grover is a Christian addictions physician who worked in Vancouver's Downtown Eastside and is a passionate defender of a harm reduction approach to addiction. In her chapter on harm reduction, she primarily defends harm reduction strategies by comparing addictive behavior to other activities that involve risk. Her primary comparison considers a friend who loves downhill skiing. In the drug use–skiing analogy, the ski resort is a "supervised site of her activity" and a ski helmet is a harm reduction device.[6] Grover also mentions children's bicycle helmets and seatbelts as examples

---

6. Grover, *Why I Help People Take Drugs*, 34.

14. RECOVERY

of harm reduction interventions.[7] She asks: If we see these risk-reducing interventions as uncomplicatedly good, why not adopt a similar approach when considering the risks associated with drug use? Grover argues that opponents of this argument view addictive behavior differently from recreational skiing because of "stigma" against pleasure, "hypocrisy," or a failure to "follow a moral logic."[8]

There may be narrow points of analogy between skiing and injecting fentanyl because of severe addiction. Both involve risk to persons, including potentially catastrophic risks. But the proverbial herd of elephants in the room of Grover's argument is the dramatic and significant ways that skiing is unlike the compulsive behavior of a person with fentanyl addiction. Most obviously, skiing is, generally speaking, a morally neutral or good activity. If we tried to imagine a perfect human society, I doubt anyone would say, "There would be no skiing there." However, I expect that almost everyone would agree that there would be no severe drug addiction in such a community.[9] There is reason other than hypocrisy or anti-pleasure stigma that we should be reluctant to facilitate addictive behaviors: these behaviors necessarily harm the persons involved.

Grover's drug use–skiing analogy reads like a classic choice-model argument. In this frame, the drug use of a person with fentanyl addiction should not be understood as significantly different from the choice of a healthy adult to go for a bicycle ride or a ski day. The differences are simply related to the ways that different individuals seek pleasure. Grover asks, "Is the pursuit of pleasure morally wrong when it applies to drugs but not when it applies to skiing?"[10] At the same time, Grover describes addiction as a

---

7. Grover, *Why I Help People Take Drugs*, 35.
8. Grover, *Why I Help People Take Drugs*, 33, 34.
9. As we have seen, this would not necessarily mean no fentanyl, which is a substance that can be used in good ways.
10. Grover, *Why I Help People Take Drugs*, 34. Even this argument in isolation cannot do the work Grover wants it to do, since lift tickets are consumer products for purchase, not government-funded healthcare initiatives.

disease, thus using the language of the disease model.[11] To hold both arguments together would require belief that her friend's skiing—and by extension any other activity involving risk—arises from a kind of brain disease. It hardly needs to be said that such an argument pathologizes a large percentage of everyday human behavior in such a way that renders the category of disease as utterly meaningless. If we do not believe that skiing is pathological because it has accordant risks, then we must accept that there is *something* different and morally complicating about what happens at, for example, a supervised consumption site.

What does all this mean? Conceptually, this suggests the need for something like a personal model of addiction. Grover's argument inadvertently demonstrates what we have already considered at length: choice and disease models are inadequate when proposed in isolation and unintelligible when proposed together. More to the point of this chapter, the weaknesses of arguments like Grover's can be summed up in their inability to consider how and why addiction necessarily harms persons. They therefore obscure the moral complexity of many harm reduction interventions.

If we want to seriously consider the morality of supervised consumption sites, we must be precise that, even at their very best, they produce both good and bad effects. Taking the devastation of addiction seriously means recognizing that the bad effects of perpetuating addictive behavior are morally significant. As such, we should devote efforts to promoting the good effects of supervised consumption sites, for example, decreased overdose and infectious disease risks. Where at all possible, we should do so in ways that avoid the unintended harmful effects of supervised consumption sites: the perpetuation of behaviors that necessarily harm persons in devastating ways. In the case of addiction, treatment aimed at recovery is a better way of decreasing both short- and long-term risks associated with addictive behavior. This suggests that harm reduction interventions are only acceptable in circumstances where the caregiver has tried to promote this higher good but is unable to do so.

11. For example: Grover, *Why I Help People Take Drugs*, 103.

14. RECOVERY

Serious consideration of the inherently harmful nature of addiction should also prompt us to think carefully about the legality of highly addictive substances. One of the many functions of law is to promote individual and community well-being by outlining which activities promote thriving for individuals and societies and which do not. A government might therefore make methamphetamine possession illegal for reasons other than a "war on drugs" that wantonly punishes persons who fundamentally need help and care. A government might make methamphetamine possession illegal for reasons other than community safety. A government might make methamphetamine possession illegal *precisely to protect and promote the health of individuals who are susceptible to developing methamphetamine addiction*. In doing so, they would be supported by evidence that legalization of drug use leads to increase in drug addiction.[12] There are important caveats to this argument. Law is inevitably a blunt and limited tool. It will usually be tempted toward retributive rather than restorative approaches, for the simple reason that restoration is more complex. Recovery is a whole-person process of body, heart, and mind that is best promoted by immersive communities of love, grace, and belonging. Legislation is a very limited tool in the creation of such spaces. But law is, among other things, a teacher about the good life. Taking the necessarily harmful nature of addiction seriously means we have reason to question policy proposals that place vulnerable persons at higher risk of developing addiction.

Does the Intervention Have a High Enough Hope for Persons?

Choice and disease models do not have a high enough view of human persons. In suggesting that addiction is fundamentally a problem of hopeless degeneracy or permanent psychopathology, they miss the ways that addiction is one expression of universal human problems: incontinent actions and disordered loves. In doing so,

12. See Cerdá et al., "Association Between Recreational Marijuana Legalization."

they ignore or obscure the factors that are most important to recovery: development of individual agency, belonging in communities of friends, and re-ordering one's life by seeking goods in more fulfilling ways. More significantly, these models miss the truth that we have good reason to hope for the meaningful recovery of addicted persons, even for those who are severely affected.

Accepting a theory with a too-low view of persons often leads to proposing action that has a too-low *hope* for persons. For example, one common argument in favor of harm-reduction approaches revolves around inevitability. If we accept that addiction is a permanent brain disease and that the person *cannot* behave in a different way, then it follows that the only possible effects of risk-reducing acts are positive. If the younger brother in the parable *cannot* return home to the Father, then maybe we fulfill our responsibility by helping him feed the pigs. In this frame, it can seem as if the only available choices are harm reduction or inaction. Grover argues, "The alternative to harm reduction is not to reduce harm. This is a passive process, a stance of inaction."[13]

There are, however, several problems with arguments that assume the inevitability of ongoing addictive behavior. First, they can lead to cynicism regarding recovery-based approaches and care models. I wonder what Grover would say about our many Christian sisters and brothers who sacrificially devote themselves toward promoting recovery from addiction within models of care that do not follow harm reduction principles. Is that passive inaction? In my own medical context, acceptance of the inevitability argument has led to disparagement of twelve-step models of care, despite the significant evidence that twelve-step communities can promote the health and well-being of vulnerable human persons. This disparaging attitude contributes to the isolation of persons with addiction by discouraging them from engaging with these communities.

Another basic problem with the inevitability argument is that it is simply untrue. As referenced in chapter 3, evidence suggests many (perhaps most) persons with addiction do recover at

13. Grover, *Why I Help People Take Drugs*, 39.

some point during their lives. It is very difficult to predict what can prompt such a journey. Hence, we should never assume that a person will continue in addictive behavior, even in an extreme circumstance. For example, I once cared for a man with a severe amphetamine addiction who had inserted a large foreign body into his rectum while intoxicated. He was subsequently unable to remove it. I believe our team offered this man the same kindness and sensitivity we strive to offer every patient we care for. But I do not remember any special or unique moment of connection or conversation. He told me he did not want to discuss his addiction. We were ultimately successful at removing the object and I discharged him. The case faded in my memory as thousands of other patients came through the emergency department. But I saw him again, many months later, for a simple muscle strain. I wrapped his knee and told him to apply ice. As I was leaving the care space, he called me back. "I wanted to tell someone one more thing. I was here a few months ago. You probably don't remember. That was a low point in my life. But everyone here was so kind to me. I couldn't believe it. It made me feel I could make a change. I wanted to tell someone that I got clean after that. I am six months sober now." The opportunity to hear about the ways small acts of kindness can dramatically change people's lives is uncommon in my work as an emergency physician. But, however rare, this patient's experience was enormously significant. His ongoing entrapment in a cycle of addiction was not inevitable. The common kindness of our nursing staff gave this man a foothold in the journey of recovery.

The deepest problem with the inevitability argument is that it fails to be adequately hopeful for persons. We have reason to hope the journey toward freedom is possible. This conclusion has concrete implications for addressing the addiction crisis. For example, I frequently speak to patients who tell me they are desperate to stop using drugs. I often read subsequent consultations from addictions clinics stating the best plan for the patient is something like "harm reduction to encourage lower risk substance use." Accepting the inevitability argument, rooted in the disease model of addiction, has produced a system that frequently offers harm reduction measures *instead of* meaningful treatment. But this approach is unjust to vulnerable persons. It does not indicate a hopeful and high view of the person. As philosopher Germain Grisez writes: "offering clean needles instead of good treatment hardly would be *fair* to drug addicts."[14] It fails to do enough for them. It fails to offer them what they are due. Grisez continues: "Public authorities should not resign themselves to the inevitability of vices such as drug abuse, regard those enslaved by them as hopeless cases, and seek only to limit further bad consequences. Rather, they should regard such a vice as a challenge to their creativity and look for constructive alternatives likely to help people live decent lives."[15]

Based on my experience, I think individual harm reduction measures can be acceptable as narrow components of a whole-person care model that aims to, and is accountable to produce, recovery from addiction. Short-term risk reduction is critically important. But it must be paired with prudent and dedicated efforts to reduce long-term risks and promote the freedom and thriving for affected persons.

To summarize, Christians should believe that it is possible for persons to achieve meaningful recovery from addiction. We should practice hope and should be critical of approaches to addiction that are essentially despairing. This does not suggest a stance of passive inaction. Rather, it calls us to a much higher standard of action, working creatively to reduce short-term risks while primarily aiming to promote meaningful recovery for suffering persons.

So What?

How can we use these two framing questions to evaluate some of the interventions that were mentioned at the beginning of this chapter? In my view, the lenses of these guiding questions directly suggest the following conclusions:

14. Grisez, "Difficult Moral Questions." Emphasis is mine.
15. Grisez, "Difficult Moral Questions."

14. RECOVERY

- Some individual harm-reduction measures—including needle exchange programs and supervised consumption sites—are acceptable if they are narrow components of a comprehensive program that aims at, and is accountable to produce, freedom from addiction. Insofar as many harm reduction programs do not have this aim, they fail to care enough about vulnerable persons. They fail to promote the highest good for them. In other words, the problem with many harm reduction programs is not that they somehow go *too far* in showing kindness or respect to persons with addiction. The problem is, in failing to assert and point toward a higher hope for persons, they do not go *far enough*. Moreover, they participate in injustice when they implicitly suggest to addicted persons that their ongoing entrapment and suffering are inevitable. I believe we should aim higher than this.

- Opioid agonist therapies (replacement medications such as Methadone and Suboxone) can and should be used as part of care for many persons with opioid addiction. They promote the good when they give persons a foothold in the journey of recovery. Because addiction is a whole-person problem, these medications are not themselves the whole solution. But, when used to satisfy physiological dependence, they can open space in the life of the person to establish patterns that displace addiction. Ideally, these medications, which do have side effects, would be weaned over time so that the person no longer had need for them. However a person who never fully weans off of these medications can still live a life of meaningful recovery.

- More generally, medical interventions that aim to address cravings and withdrawal can be important to promoting the good for persons with addiction. These interventions include medical management of alcohol withdrawal to reduce seizure risk and nicotine replacement strategies. These are ideally employed with the clear aim of producing recovery and alongside whole-person interventions that can do so.

Physicians and nurses have the gift of caring for persons in these vulnerable moments, and the accordant weighty responsibility to foster the things that promote recovery more than any medication: human connection, reconciliation, mutual respect, and hope.

- Residential treatment facilities generally aim to produce recovery from addiction. Ideally, these facilities would prudently use narrow medical tools while investing in whole-person care. They most successfully promote recovery when they demonstrate a high view of persons by investing in mentorship, vocational discernment, personal development, and enjoyment of the beautiful.

- Twelve-step programs take the necessarily harmful nature of addiction seriously. In addition, rich twelve-step communities demonstrate a high hope for persons by investing heavily in them. This hope is substantiated by the many people who have found recovery through these communities. As such, and despite some potential points of difference, I believe that Christians should see twelve-step programs as spaces that often promote recovery and have a high view of persons. Not everyone needs a twelve-step community to recover. However, when giving advice to persons with addiction, Christians should encourage participation in these communities as potentially extremely helpful.

- The tools of law should be judiciously used to teach that certain behaviors are necessarily contrary to individual and community thriving. As such, a legal framework that recognizes the harm of addiction and has a high view of persons will seek to protect those who may be susceptible to developing addiction. Christians can support laws that promote the good without believing that law is the primary teacher of morality or the primary vehicle of recovery for persons with addiction. Rather, Christians should invest in thick moral and social spaces that can do what laws cannot: provide friendship, affection, meaning, and belonging to persons seeking recovery.

14. RECOVERY

The questions of whether an intervention recognizes the harm of addiction and has a high view of persons can similarly be applied to help Christians parse other proposed ways of addressing addiction. This particular Christian approach cannot make sense if coming from the sidelines. It is only intelligible when coming from a community of persons that is itself going further by investing in physical and social spaces that witness to the truth that there is reason for a higher hope. Doing so is difficult and costly. Doing so is the necessary task of the church.

15. Hope

The church should be a place of hope, because we trust in God's power to make all things new.

ONE OF MY FAVORITE stories about addiction begins like a parable:

> Once on Mount Athos, there was a monk who lived in Karyes. He drank and got drunk every day and was the cause of the scandal to the pilgrims. Eventually he died and this relieved some of the faithful who went on to tell Elder Paisios that they were delighted that the huge problem was finally solved. Father Paisios answered them that he knew about the death of the monk, after seeing the entire battalion of angels who came to collect his soul. The pilgrims were amazed and some of them protested and tried to explain to the Elder of whom they were talking about, thinking that the Elder did not understand.[1]

The Elder then related to the gathered pilgrims the life of the addicted monk. Sadly, he had been frequently given alcohol by his parents as a child and therefore developed a severe addiction. As a young man, he came to the monastery and confessed to the Elder that he could not escape his addiction. The Elder invited him to join in the religious life of the faith community. The Elder instructed him to pray for God's intervention to help him "reduce by one the glasses he drank. After a year he managed with struggle

---

1. Sanidopoulos, "Elder Paisios and the Alcoholic Monk."

and repentance to make the twenty glasses he drank into nineteen glasses. The struggle continued over the years and he reached two to three glasses, with which he would still get drunk."[2] The monk died without achieving sobriety, without entering what most people in the contemporary addiction conversation would call recovery. Most of his own religious community viewed his life as a failure. An embarrassment, even. But the Elder was gifted the eyes to see the ways in which this monk's path was a beautiful journey toward God. Like all of us, the monk died without being fully free of bondage to sin and suffering. But God was the one who saw behind the addictive behavior and treasured the devoted effort of the person. "The world for years saw an alcoholic monk who scandalized the pilgrims, but God saw a fighter."[3]

The final word in any Christian conversation about addiction should be about the hope we have in God. Loss of hope, despair, pervades the present public dialogue around addiction. This has roots in views of addiction that fail to be hopeful enough for persons. But despair is often also deeply rooted in people's experience. Working in a place like St. Paul's emergency department means regularly confronting the terrifying power of a variety of addictions. It means confronting our own helplessness, as we realize how little the medical system can do to help our patients. If we are honest, it means confronting our own entrapment in patterns of disorder and incontinence. It is not surprising that many caregivers are tempted to despair and accept insufficient interventions that presume the inevitability of addictive behavior. What these colleagues and conversation partners need, more than anything, is hope. They need cheerful and patient friends who bear witness to a different way, whose lives justify a hopeful outlook. They need the example of communities where lives are changed and freedom is found. The core task of the church is to be this kind of place.

We have already considered how the personal model of addiction suggests that we should hope for meaningful recovery of persons with addiction. Christians should believe that severe addiction

2. Sanidopoulos, "Elder Paisios and the Alcoholic Monk."
3. Sanidopoulos, "Elder Paisios and the Alcoholic Monk."

can be displaced through the power of a cooperative effort between the agency of the person, the love of gracious communities, and the virtue-infusing work of the Holy Spirit. We should work toward this outcome in our own lives and in the lives of all those we encounter with addiction. We should never aim lower. At the same time, the Christian truth that all our stories are only fulfilled in eternal union with God allows us to have confident hope for persons who do not escape from the entrapping power of addiction in this life. As such, and as a blessing to those who have died in places like St. Paul's Hospital, I want to conclude with a reflection on our high hope for persons who never "enter recovery." Persons like the alcoholic monk. Persons like Miles.

Addiction, Death, and the Welcome of God

I recently stood beside a man named Miles as he was dying. I knew Miles quite well. I knew the ways addiction had undermined his vocations, his relationships, and his health. I knew some of the ways he had tried to find freedom from its entrapping power, without success. I knew the ways that his addiction was directly leading to his death at a young age. The prior evening, the critical care team had determined that further interventions were medically futile. They had called Miles's family to let them know he was dying. Multiple family members lived a relatively short distance from the hospital, but they did not want to come and see him. And so, Miles was dying alone. One of the nurses had gently bundled him up in blankets to keep his frail body warm in his last moments. "Like a baby," she said to me. I stood at his bedside. Instead of being faithfully present and focused on the person in front of me, I allowed myself to be distracted and angry. I could not believe that the journey of Miles's life would end this way, that no one loved him enough to be with him at the end. I left his bedside and called his father again. He said he "would try to come in later." When I returned, Miles's nurse told me he had died while I was on the phone. She had been out of the room as well, caring for a critically ill patient. I could not believe Miles died alone.

15. HOPE

Because I am a Christian, I believe it is right to rebel against the factors, including his severe addiction, that lead to such a premature and lonely death. Miles was a person, made in the image of God and therefore deserving of respect and reverence. This is *why* his suffering was so deeply tragic. This is why it is right for us to spend our lives caring for persons like him.

To be a Christian is to say more than this. To be a Christian is to know he was not alone. Someone did love him enough to be with him at the end. He was joined, even in a lonely death, by the God whose all-power is power to mend us, whose infinite freedom is freedom to join us to the divine life, and whose beauty is sufficient to glorify our scars. To be a Christian is to say, *especially* through the vale of tears, that all will be well for Miles. All of his tears will be wiped away.

Everyone I have ever talked to about addiction is morally outraged at the suffering it can cause. Everyone agrees that things *should* be different. For the Christian, this moral rebellion is grounded in a belief that things *will* be different. The journey of a person with addiction does not end in a binary: either fully recovered success or utter failure. The journey of a person with addiction ends in the God who hates injustice, who blesses the meek and the hungry, who counts our tears, and who created us for eternal freedom. The work of persons to free themselves from addiction is treasured by God, even if they do not fully escape their addiction in this lifetime. The Christian has hope, as the Epistle says, that "the one who began a good work in you will continue to complete it until the day of Jesus Christ."[4] Apart from belief in something very much like the Christian God, Miles's story is simply one of fathomless tragedy. He was alone at the end. But the Christian God is the *One* who will vindicate and fulfill the beautiful things about Miles's life. The work of Christ will last into eternity, so Miles's efforts toward the good, true, and beautiful will endure. Christ died alone, so Miles was joined by God, even at the end. Christ's palms have scars on them, so Miles's wounds can be healed and glorified. Christ was raised, so Miles will be raised. Amen.

4. Phil 1:6.

I have seen her as a patient many times. Overdoses. Withdrawal. Self-inflicted burns. Sometimes she has given no discernible medical reason to be in the emergency department at all. Sometimes she has taken a swing at a staff member from her wheelchair: a surprisingly powerful punch from someone who seems so frail. Sometimes she just sits and cries inconsolably in the waiting room.

People say things about her. That she is actually a big-time drug dealer with high-level gang connections. That she didn't used to be so mean, or that she used to be even meaner.

I have seen her as a patient many times. And then I did not see her anymore. For our patients with severe opioid addictions, that usually means they are in jail or dead. We mourned her absence in our way, adding her to the list of former frequent presenters that we meditate on in quiet moments on night shifts:

"Remember Pat? We used to call him Elvis, because he would come in drunk and sing love songs in Triage Hall. What was his last name again? I heard he's dead now."

"Did you ever see that guy Gabriel? When he was on meth he would take more sedation than anyone I've ever seen. He'd fight four security guards at once. But at other times he was the sweetest guy. He just wanted to get back to Mexico to see his mom again. I wonder if he ever did."

"And Wendy Forrest? She was here every night for months. Went to ICU a few times. I don't think anyone knows what happened to her."

I did not see her for a long time. And then, in the closest I have ever come to having a religious vision, I did. I was walking across Granville Street after an early morning shift. So much suffering. My head was down. I would like to say I was praying, but I wasn't.

I heard music. I looked up. A man was playing a saxophone on the corner of Granville and Georgia. The air was thick with jazz and the smell from a nearby hot dog cart. The cart had a bubble machine on it, which sent soapy spheres floating lazily over the tiny crowd of people who had stopped to listen, smell, and taste.

And there she was. I saw her before she saw me. She was sitting in the midst of all this, watching, listening, and clapping her hands. A half-eaten hot dog sat on her lap. She was smiling broadly, alive as I had never imagined possible, transfixed by the beauty of the music and consumed by the wonder of the moment. Delighted. In that moment, this world tasted its destiny. Lions will lay with lambs. Swords will be beat into plowshares. And Wendy will be eternally free.

She saw me, waved, and beckoned me to join her.

Bibliography

Abdul-Quader, Abu S., et al. "Effectiveness of Structural-Level Needle/Syringe Programs to Reduce HCV and HIV Infection Among People Who Inject Drugs: A Systematic Review." *AIDS and Behavior* 17.2 (2013) 878–92.
Alcoholics Anonymous. *Alcoholics Anonymous Big Book*. Charleston, SC: BN Publishing, 2008.
Alexander, Bruce K. *The Globalization of Addiction: A Study in Poverty of the Spirit*. Oxford: Oxford University Press, 2010.
Alexander, Bruce K., and Anton R. F. Schweighofer. "Defining 'Addiction.'" *Canadian Psychology/Psychologie Canadienne* 29 (1988) 151–62.
American Psychiatric Association. *Diagnostic and Statistical Manual of Mental Disorders*. 5th ed. Arlington, VA: American Psychiatric Association, 2013.
Aristotle. *The Nicomachean Ethics*. Translated by J. A. K. Thomson. Rev. ed. London: Penguin, 2004.
Bird, Kathleen, et al. "Clinicians' Perspectives and an Ethical Analysis of Safer Supply Opioid Prescribing." *Journal of Bioethical Inquiry* n.d. (2024) n.d.
Bourdain, Anthony. *Kitchen Confidential: Adventures in the Culinary Underbelly*. London: Bloomsbury, 2013.
British Columbia Ministry of Mental Health and Addictions. "Escalating BC's Response to the Overdose Emergency." February 2019. https://www2.gov.bc.ca/assets/gov/overdose-awareness/mmha_escalating_bcs_response_report_final_26feb.pdf.
Camosy, Charles C. *Losing Our Dignity: How Secularized Medicine Is Undermining Fundamental Human Equality*. Hyde Park, NY: New City, 2021.
———. *Resisting Throwaway Culture: How a Consistent Life Ethic Can Unite a Fractured People*. Hyde Park, NY: New City, 2019.

Carson, Marion L. S. "Freedom and Its Anxieties: Incongruous Grace and Innovative Communities in Pastoral Perspective." In *The New Perspective on Grace: Paul and the Gospel After Paul and the Gift*, edited by Edward Adams et al., 301–15. Grand Rapids, MI: Eerdmans, 2023.

Castro, Jordan. "Recovering from Heroin and Fiction." *Plough Quarterly*, September 17, 2024. https://www.plough.com/en/topics/faith/recovering-from-heroin-and-fiction.

Cerdá, Magdalena, et al. "Association Between Recreational Marijuana Legalization in the United States and Changes in Marijuana Use and Cannabis Use Disorder from 2008 to 2016." *Journal of the American Medical Association Psychiatry* 77 (2019) 165–71.

Dalrymple, Theodore. "Stigma and Sympathy." Law and Liberty, September 18, 2020. https://lawliberty.org/stigma-and-sympathy/.

Denizet-Lewis, Benoit. "An Anti-Addiction Pill?" *The New York Times Magazine*, June 25, 2006. https://www.nytimes.com/2006/06/25/magazine/an-anti addiction-pill.html.

De Quincey, Thomas. *Confessions of an English Opium-Eater*. London: Arcturus, 2019.

Dostoevsky, Fyodor. *The Brothers Karamazov*. Edited by Susan McReynolds Oddo and translated by Constance Garnett. New York: Norton, 2011.

Dunnington, Kent. *Addiction and Virtue: Beyond the Models of Disease and Choice*. Downers Grove, IL: InterVarsity Academic, 2011.

Elster, Jon. *Strong Feelings*. Cambridge, MA: MIT Press, 2000.

Foddy, Bennett, and Julian Savulescu. "A Liberal Account of Addiction." *Philosophy, Psychiatry, and Psychology* 17 (2010) 1–22.

Forsyth, Mark. *A Short History of Drunkenness*. London: Penguin, 2018.

Genuis, Quentin. "Dignity Reevaluated: A Theological Examination of Human Dignity and the Role of the Church in Bioethics and End-of-Life Care." *The Linacre Quarterly* 83 (2016) 6–14.

Gleichgerrcht, Ezequiel, and Jean Decety. "The Relationship Between Different Facets of Empathy, Pain Perception and Compassion Fatigue Among Physicians." *Frontiers in Behavioral Neuroscience* 8 (2014) n.d.

Government of British Columbia. "Stop Overdose." https://www.stopoverdose.gov.bc.ca/.

Greene, Graham. *Brighton Rock*. New York: Penguin, 2020.

Grisel, Judith. *Never Enough: The Neuroscience and Experience of Addiction*. Melbourne: Scribe, 2019.

Grisez, Germain. "Difficult Moral Questions, Question 196: Should the City Council Vote to Supply Needles to Drug Addicts?" The Way of the Lord Jesus. http://twotlj.org/G-3-196.html.

Grover, Meera Bai. *Why I Help People Take Drugs: Reflections of a Christian Addiction Medicine Physician*. Eugene, OR: Cascade, 2024.

Hari, Johann. "Everything You Think You Know About Addiction Is Wrong." Ted.com, June 2015. https://www.ted.com/talks/johann_hari_everything_you_think_you_know_about_addiction_is_wrong?language=en.

Hauerwas, Stanley. "Abortion, Theologically Understood." In *On Moral Medicine: Theological Perspectives in Medical Ethics*, edited by M. Therese Lysaught and Joseph J. Kotva Jr., 945–53. Grand Rapids, MI: Eerdmans, 2012.

———. "Salvation and Health: Why Medicine Needs the Church." In *On Moral Medicine: Theological Perspectives in Medical Ethics*, edited by M. Therese Lysaught and Joseph J. Kotva Jr., 43–51. Grand Rapids, MI: Eerdmans, 2012.

Heyman, Gene M. "How Individuals Make Choices Explains Addiction's Distinctive, Non-Eliminable Features." *Behavioural Brain Research* 397 (2021) 112899.

Illich, Ivan. *Limits to Medicine: Medical Nemesis, the Expropriation of Health*. London: M. Boyars, 1995.

Jacob's Well. "Our Vision and Values." https://www.jacobswell.ca/vision-values.

Jung, Carl G. *C.G. Jung Letters, Volume 2*. Edited by Gerhard Adler and Aniela Jaffé. Translated by R. F. C. Hull. Repr., Princeton, NJ: Princeton University Press, 2021.

Kaskutas, Lee Ann. "Alcoholics Anonymous Effectiveness: Faith Meets Science." *Journal of Addictive Diseases* 28 (2009) 145–57.

Keller, Timothy. *The Prodigal God: Recovering the Heart of the Christian Faith*. New York: Penguin, 2008.

Kelly, John F., et al. "Alcoholics Anonymous and Other 12-Step Programs for Alcohol Use Disorder." *Cochrane Database of Systematic Reviews* 3 (2020) n.d.

Kennedy-Hendricks, Alene, et al. "Experience of Personal Loss Due to Drug Overdose Among US Adults." *JAMA Health Forum* 5 (2024) e241262.

Kingsolver, Barbara. *Demon Copperhead*. New York: Harper, 2022.

Klingemann, Harald, et al. "Continuities and Changes in Self-Change Research." *Addiction* 105 (2009) 1510–18.

Knapp, Caroline. *Drinking: A Love Story*. New York: The Dial, 1997.

Lankenau, Stephen E., et al. "Initiation into Prescription Opioid Misuse Amongst Young Injection Drug Users." *International Journal of Drug Policy* 23 (2012) 37–44.

Lembke, Anna. *Dopamine Nation: Finding Balance in the Age of Indulgence*. New York: Penguin, 2021.

Levine, H. G. "The Discovery of Addiction: Changing Conceptions of Habitual Drunkenness in America." *Journal of Studies on Alcohol* 39 (1978) 143–74.

Levy, Neil. "Addiction Is Not a Brain Disease (and It Matters)." *Frontiers in Psychiatry* 4 (2013) 1–24.

Lewis, C. S. *They Asked for a Paper*. London: Geoffrey Bles, 1962.

Lookatch, Samantha J., et al. "Effects of Social Support and 12-Step Involvement on Recovery Among People in Continuing Care for Cocaine Dependence." *Substance Use and Misuse* 54 (2019) 2144–55.

MacIntyre, Alasdair. *Dependent Rational Animals: Why Human Beings Need the Virtues*. Chicago: Open Court, 1999.

BIBLIOGRAPHY

Marlowe, Ann. *How to Stop Time: Heroin from A to Z.* London: Virago, 2002.

Marshall, Brandon D. L., et al. "Reduction in Overdose Mortality After the Opening of North America's First Medically Supervised Safer Injecting Facility: A Retrospective Population-Based Study." *The Lancet* 377 (2011) 1429–37.

Marshall, Bruce. *The World, the Flesh and Fr. Smith.* Repr., Manchester, NH: Sophia Institute Press, 2023.

Maté, Gabor. "Beyond Drugs: The Universal Experience of Addiction." Dr. Gabor Maté, April 5, 2017. https://drgabormate.com/opioids-universal-experience-addiction/.

———. *In the Realm of Hungry Ghosts: Close Encounters with Addiction.* London: Vermilion, 2018.

May, Gerald G. *Addiction and Grace: Love and Spirituality in the Healing of Addictions.* San Francisco: HarperOne, 2007.

Meilaender, Gilbert. *Neither Beast Nor God: The Dignity of the Human Person.* New York: Encounter, 2009.

Modi, Hemel Narendra, et al. "A Decade of Imaging Surgeons' Brain Function (Part II): A Systematic Review of Applications for Technical and Nontechnical Skills Assessment." *Surgery* 162 (2017) 1130–39.

Moltmann, Jürgen. "Christianity: A Religion of Joy." In *Joy and Human Flourishing: Essays on Theology, Culture, and the Good Life*, edited by Miroslav Volf and Justin E. Crisp, 1–14. Minneapolis: Fortress, 2015.

Nietzsche, Friedrich. "The Antichrist." In *The Portable Nietzsche*, edited and translated by Walter Kaufmann, 565–656. New York: Penguin, 1982.

Nouwen, Henri. *Reaching Out: The Three Movements of the Spiritual Life.* London: Fount, 1996.

O'Donovan, Oliver. "Again, Who Is a Person?" In *On Moral Medicine: Theological Perspectives in Medical Ethics*, edited by M. Therese Lysaught and Joseph J. Kotva Jr., 367–71. Grand Rapids, MI: Eerdmans, 2012.

Peele, Stanton. "The Seductive, But Dangerous, Allure of Gabor Maté." *Psychology Today*, December 5, 2011. https://www.psychologytoday.com/us/blog/addiction-in-society/201112/the-seductive-dangerous-allure-gabor-mat.

Quinones, Sam. *Dreamland: The True Tale of America's Opiate Epidemic.* New York: Bloomsbury, 2015.

Regnerus, Mark, et al. "Documenting Pornography Use in America: A Comparative Analysis of Methodological Approaches." *The Journal of Sex Research* 53 (2015) 873–81.

Sanidopoulos, John. "Elder Paisios and the Alcoholic Monk." Orthodox Christianity Then and Now, 2012. https://www.johnsanidopoulos.com/2012/03/elder-paisios-and-alcoholic-monk.html.

Schaff, Philip, ed. *Nicene and Post-Nicene Fathers. First Series.* New York: Cosimo Classics, 2007.

Schaler, Jeffrey A. *Addiction Is a Choice.* Chicago: Open Court, 2000.

Sheff, David. *Beautiful Boy: A Father's Journey Through His Son's Addiction.* Boston: Houghton Mifflin, 2008.

Sheff, Nic. *Tweak: Growing Up on Methamphetamines.* New York: Atheneum Books for Young Readers, 2007.

Smith, James K. A. *On the Road with Saint Augustine: A Real-World Spirituality for Restless Hearts.* Grand Rapids, MI: Brazos, 2019.

———. *You Are What You Love: The Spiritual Power of Habit.* Grand Rapids, MI: Brazos, 2016.

Smithwick, Tom. *Knocking on Freedom's Door: Hope Filled Stories of Addiction Recovery and Healing.* Self-published, 2021.

Spufford, Francis. *Unapologetic: Why, Despite Everything, Christianity Can Still Make Surprising Emotional Sense.* New York: HarperCollins, 2013.

Vancouver, City of. "Downtown Eastside." https://vancouver.ca/news-calendar/downtown-eastside.aspx.

Wallace, David Foster. *Infinite Jest: A Novel.* Boston: Little, Brown and Company, 1996.

Welch, Edward T. "A Letter to an Alcoholic." *The Journal of Biblical Counseling* 16 (1998) 19–26.

———. "Self-Control: The Battle Against 'One More.'" *The Journal of Biblical Counseling* 19 (2001) 24–31.

Wexler, Arnie, et al. *All Bets Are Off: Losers, Liars, and Recovery from Gambling Addiction.* Las Vegas: Central Recovery, 2014.

White, Aaron. *Recovering: From Brokenness and Addiction to Blessedness and Community.* Grand Rapids, MI: Baker Academic, 2020.

Williams, Rowan. *Faith in the Public Square.* London: Bloomsbury Continuum, 2015.

Wilson, Gary. *Your Brain on Porn: Internet Pornography and the Emerging Science of Addiction.* Margate, Kent: Commonwealth, 2014.

Wiman, Christian. *Zero at the Bone: Fifty Entries Against Despair.* New York: Farrar, Straus and Giroux, 2023.

Wolterstorff, Nicholas. *Lament for a Son.* Grand Rapids, MI: Eerdmans, 1987.

Zahl, David. *Low Anthropology: The Unlikely Key to a Gracious View of Others (and Yourself).* Grand Rapids, MI: Brazos, 2022.

Subject Index

agency, personal, 23–24, 42, 107–11
Alcoholics Anonymous. *See* twelve step programs
Alexander, Bruce, 18n1, 27n14, 57n6
Aristotle, 52–54
Augustine, Saint, 43–45, 88, 113
autonomy, personal, 88–89

burnout, 117–21

Camosy, Charles, 88–89
compassion, 117–21
culpability, 37–40, 42

Dalrymple, Theodore, 22, 38–39
De Quincey, Thomas, 15–16
Demon Copperhead (book), 56–57
determinism, 28–30
Dostoevsky, Fyodor, 26, 67
Dunnington, Kent, 15, 20, 52, 103–4

Elster, Jon, 46

friendship, 92–94

Greene, Graham, 75–76

Grisel, Judith, 5n4, 50, 97
Grisez, Germaine, 134
Grover, Meera, 95n2, 128–32

Hari, Johann, 48
harm reduction, 127–37
Hauerwas, Stanley, 89, 119
hospitality, 90–92

Illich, Ivan, 119
Infinite Jest (book), 51
Jung, Carl, 96

Keller, Tim, 70, 72, 74
Knapp, Caroline, 27

Levine, Harry, 18
Levy, Neil, 31
Lewis, C.S., 46–47

MacIntyre, Alasdair, 89
Marlowe, Ann, 27, 46, 48
Maté, Gabor 24–25, 32, 55, 95–96
May, Gerald, 7n10
Meilaender, Gilbert, 16

SUBJECT INDEX

needle exchange programs, *see* harm reduction
Nietzsche, Friedrich, 118
Nouwen, Henri, 90

O'Donovan, Oliver, 17
opioid agonist therapy, 135
personhood, significance of, 16–17, 79

safe injection sites. *See* harm reduction
Savulescu, Julian, 19, 24
Schaler, Jeffrey, 19
Sheff, David, 116
sin, 100–105

Smith, James K. A., 43–44, 113

"throwaway culture" (concept), 88–89
twelve step programs, 49, 98, 103, 125–26, 136

virtue ethics, 53
voluntarism, 18–20

White, Aaron, 50n1, 75
Williams, Rowan, 123
Wiman, Christian, 110–12
Wolterstoff, Nicholas, 119
worship, addiction as, 46

www.ingramcontent.com/pod-product-compliance
Lightning Source LLC
Chambersburg PA
CBHW022119160426
43197CB00009B/1089